16.99 *

NEW FOOD
for a
VEGETARIAN
FAMILY

NEW FOOD
for a
VEGETARIAN FAMILY

SIMON HOPE

Photography by Sara Taylor

MITCHELL BEAZLEY

First published in Great Britain in 1995
by Mitchell Beazley
an imprint of Reed Consumer Books Limited
Michelin House, 81 Fulham Road,
London SW3 6RB
and Auckland, Melbourne, Singapore
and Toronto

ISBN 1 85732 501 X

A CIP catalogue record for this book is available at the British Library.

Printed in Hong Kong

ACKNOWLEDGEMENTS

Art Director Jacqui Small
Designer Barbara Zuniga
Executive Editor Susan Haynes
Editor Kathy Steer
Production Controller Melanie Frantz
Photographer Sara Taylor
Home Economist Louise Pickford
Stylist Wei Tang

NOTES

Both metric and imperial measurements
have been given in all recipes.

Use one set of measurements only and not
a mixture of both.

Standard level spoon measurements are
used in all recipes.
1 tablespoon = one 15 ml spoon
1 teaspoon = one 5 ml spoon

Eggs should be free range and size 3 unless
otherwise stated.
Milk should be full -fat unless otherwise
stated.
Shoyu is Japanese Soy Sauce
Nibbed is tiny dice.

Ovens should be preheated to the specified
temperature - if using a fan assisted oven,
follow the manufacturer's instructions for
adjusting the time and temperature.

I'd like to say a big thank you to my family especially Kate for bravely cooking where no one has cooked before. To Daisy for honesty, Hamish for his tastebuds and Mollie for eating up everything on her plate!

CONTENTS

INTRODUCTION

Don't worry, you're normal, you have a healthy interest in good food, you may or may not be vegetarian but one thing for sure; you care. Picking up this book and getting so far deserves a reward, now read on, you're in good company.

I have been in the vegetarian restaurant business now for 18 years – almost all of my working life – and I still love it and the food we create. But unlike when I started I now have a family of my own. Three times Kate has grown large; successfully given birth and breastfed our children – Daisy, Hamish and Mollie. Three times she has produced the most delightful, happy, healthy and vibrant offspring. 'Not bad for a vegetarian' some people say, as if the only sure way of breeding healthy humans is on a diet of meat and fish.

It became obvious to me that a cookbook was needed for families, a book to banish the misconceptions inbred by a meat-obsessed society, a book to turn the tables and suggest that it is probably best not to eat meat when pregnant and breastfeeding. It is far healthier and less dangerous to have a meat-free diet so long as your vegetarian diet is fully comprehensive. Human beings were definitely never designed to eat so much meat, let alone meat that comes from animals pumped with chemicals and growth hormones. A pregnant or breastfeeding mother should eat food as pure as possible. *New Food for a Vegetarian Family* probes to the very heart of family catering, covering the practicalities of feeding a vegetarian family through the early years and on to school and out the other side.

I'm a great lover of France (although the French, in general, have absolutely no concept of vegetarian food) and a few years ago I dropped in at a convenient farmhouse to buy a few litres of local plonk. At the huge kitchen table worked an equally huge woman filling yards of intestine with ground pork to make huge sausages. In my broken French I managed a reasonably humorous and, I thought, eloquent conversation the gist of which was about their pig which they had killed three weeks earlier and these last bits of it were going into the sausages. Such sound and frugal housekeeping has more in common with life in the 17th century than today: they killed their pig because they needed the meat and you can bet your last nut cutlet that not one part of the animal was wasted or unappreciated.

The number of people in England today who are wholly or partly vegetarian or vegan is growing at a meteoric rate and it is not just because they don't like the idea of eating animals. Often it has got more to do with a dislike of how the animal has been reared, what it was given to eat, what drugs made it grow larger and leaner, what it tastes like and whether our bodies really need it. It is not generally our pig, after all.

I have a lot of friends who, on principle, would never touch vegetarian food – they 'like their meat'. A closer examination shows that these people actually don't like their meat. Unlike the French farmer's wife, who valued her pig (and every last bit of it, too) these so called 'carnivores' balk at any part of the animal that doesn't come neatly wrapped in a supermarket package clearly designed to minimize the chance of them actually having to touch the real thing. It has always seemed strangely paradoxical to me that most carnivores will happily eat a cow's bottom but not its head. And when it comes to cooking, what do these meat eaters do to their meat? They render it tasteless by overcooking it.

If the truth be known, We're a nation of vegetarians waiting to come out of the closet. We've lost touch with animal husbandry and we are frightened of being shown the level and types of slaughter that take place every day so that we can overcook this meat.

In the past, people fought for meat, but then it was a rare treat. Meat symbolized health, wealth, happiness and security in a time when life itself was more uncertain. For the common people it was often an unobtainable goal which, if achieved, was seen as a buffer against the harsh physical existence of a world in which there were no luxuries or labour-saving devices.

The 20th century has brought with it plenty of meat for us Westerners, as well as every luxury and labour-saving device. The symbolic desire for meat has remained intact but the actual need has completely disappeared. Consequently,

meat itself has become a killer – heart disease, bowel disease and obesity have become the biggest threat to us – far more so than AIDS. Is it any surprise that so many people are becoming vegetarian? If meat ever becomes popular again, it'll be because some future society will ensure that we all have our own pig or cow to tend, love and finally eat.

In writing this book I have talked to parents whose children suffer from a wide variety of illnesses from simple allergies, through asthma to autism. Without exception they all wish they had appreciated the importance of diet before having children, theres not a lot we can do about our genetic structure (yet), but we can get the best from our bodies by altering by what we eat and especially when pregnant and in the vital first 18 months after birth, during which our vital organs develop along with our immune systems. Nowadays it is very easy for pregnant women and young mothers to opt for nutritious diets which are full of organic foods that are particularly designed for their own bodies.

I hope you enjoy *New Food for a Vegetarian Family*. I've had great fun writing it and I hope that it will help you and your family have a happier and healthier life.

EQUIPMENT, COOKING TECHNIQUES AND INGREDIENTS

EQUIPMENT

Knives

Use the right knife for you and life as a vegetarian cook will be more fun. On the whole vegetarians have to prepare more vegetables and fruit than their meat-eating counterparts who can just slam a rib on to the 'barbie', sit back and relax.

I use a Japanese vegetable chopping knife. It has a square nose, a good balance and is very sharp. Our Head Chef, Karen, at 'Food For Friends', prefers a huge pointed knife.

Practise chopping vegetables like courgettes or cucumbers with the fingers of the non-knife wielding hand tucked well in, while at the same time keeping the vegetable or fruit firmly in place. Let the last knuckle of the middle finger act as a guide against which the knife goes up and down.

Vegetables and fruits will be cut according to their role in the dish, be it to lie flat, stand square or just look pretty. Always wash them well before use, except mushrooms which should just be brushed to remove any dirt (water makes mushrooms soggy). Waxed fruits like oranges should be scrubbed first in hot water, if the rind is to be used. Waxed cucumbers must have their skins removed, unless organically grown – the wax holds in chemical sprays. Remove all damaged or blighted parts of the fruit or vegetable. Knives must be sharpened, preferably after each use to maintain a perfect edge. Equally after use they should be stored very carefully on a magnetic strip or in a wooden block to avoid damaging their sharpness.

Pots and Pans

Keep pots and pans clean and dry. Most metal dishes start to suffer metal fatigue simply because they are not dried properly. If they don't have plastic handles the best way to dry them is in the oven. It is a very tempting but false economy to buy cheap cookware. Thick gauge stainless steel lined with copper will last a lifetime although it is not necessary in the case of pans for boiling or steaming. Burnt pots should be scoured only with salt and lemon juice.

Cooking Vegetables and Fruit

The art of cooking vegetables is to preserve their flavour, texture and nutritional benefits. Generally fruit preparation should be done at the last moment as fruit is prone to lose water, shape and colour very quickly after preparation.

These are several different cooking techniques involved as described below.

Boiling

Boiling is a technique used less and less. First bring lightly salted water to the boil, add the unfortunate vegetables and bring to the boil again before reducing the heat to a gentle rolling boil. Remove the vegetables before they are tender as they will continue to cook afterwards. Save the liquid to use as stock or for cooking more vegetables.

Steaming

Steaming is much more in vogue these days as the end result has greater flavour and higher nutrients. Buy a cheap bamboo Chinese system that will fit one of your pans. Different liquids will give the subject of steaming subtly different flavours.

Stir-frying or sautéing

These are probably the most common methods used in vegetarian cookery. Heat the pan first, add the oil or butter and remove from the heat if very hot, to avoid burning. Toss and stir the vegetables into the oil or butter and make sure each is evenly coated. The combination of hot oil and hot pan will for a time seal in the flavour of the vegetables. If you are not able to toss the vegetables in the pan use a wooden spoon and stir them.

Roasting

This is definitely the most up and coming technique in vegetarian cookery. In the past only root vegetables and certain bulbs were commonly roasted. Now aubergines, peppers, courgettes, tomatoes, onions, shallots, garlic, fennel and even asparagus are quite commonly roasted. The basic rules apply. Vegetables have very little natural fat so more must be added, any oil will do but I like extra virgin olive oil best. Try adding your favourite dried herbs and seasonings. Heat a little oil in a roasting tin, brush the vegetables to be roasted with oil and sprinkle on salt and pepper and anything else you fancy. Quickly sauté on the top of the stove before putting into a hot oven. Some people peel roasted peppers and aubergines but unless they are completely blackened I can't see the point. When roasting garlic it is best to use fresh garlic.

Ingredients

Herbs

Always use fresh herbs when available. Soft leafy herbs like basil are best added at the end of the cooking process while 'hard' leaves like bay are best added at the beginning. Smaller-leaved fresh herbs can be added whenever called for. Dried herbs should be revitalized by rubbing between the palms of your hand – this reactivates the enriched oils in them and helps bring more flavour to the dish. Always keep dried herbs in a cool dark place and fresh herbs like flowers in a vase of water.

Spices

If using freshly ground spices grind them in a coffee mill dedicated to spices and clean out thoroughly after each use. Ready-ground spices must be kept cool and in a dark place or jar. Ground spices are fat-soluble and so must always be added at the stir-fry stage of a dish. Pepper is a spice and you should use freshly ground black pepper.

Dried beans, pulses and grains

Most beans and some pulses should be well soaked before cooking. Cooking times will vary according to how long they have been soaked and how old they are.

Garlic

Once a week peel a whole bulb or two of garlic and keep covered with extra virgin olive oil. Not only do you then have instant fresh garlic, you also have at the end of the week garlic-flavoured olive oil – yummy!

Leeks, watercress and spinach

These are notoriously dirty vegetables so take great care to wash them thoroughly – be quick preparing spinach or use iced water as it does wilt quickly.

Green potatoes

If you're pregnant or breastfeeding do not eat green potatoes.

Cream

Sauces made with cream are a lovely treat. Remember that as vegetarians you probably eat 50% less fat than meat eaters anyway. If you can get it use organic cream.

STORAGE AND NUTRITIONAL CONSIDERATIONS

Storage

Quite simply 'fresh is best' but a little careful handling can extend the life of fruit and vegetables. They are best stored in a cool dark place. Light and heat destroy their delicate system which begins to decay the moment they are picked. Throw out all glass storage jars and replace them with tins or pottery jars. If possible keep excess vegetables in the garage or cellar; funnily enough, refrigerators can hasten the demise of fruit and vegetables as much as heat. Three to four days is the maximum length of time for which most vegetables or fruits can be refrigerated. Never refrigerate potatoes, bananas or citrus fruits, unless cut.

With the exception of frozen peas, sweetcorn, broad beans and some of the summer fruits, freezers are best used for finished products such as ready-made meals, sauces, purées and stocks.

Some fruits and vegetables are best preserved in oil or vinegar, or simply sun-dried. In these cases they usually take on a new identity and become more of an ingredient than they were originally.

Nutrition

Proteins: vegetarians get protein from many sources but I believe the best source is a combination of beans, grains and cereals.

Fats: don't use margarines, use butter or cold-pressed extra virgin olive oils. Butter is a completely natural product and if eaten in small quantities can do no harm. Margarines are altogether different – I'm sure that the manufacturing techniques, even of pure vegetable margarines is suspect. (Remember that fat children become fat adults.)

Vitamins and minerals: to ensure a good intake of vitamins and minerals simply eat good fresh and varied food that has been cooked at home. Do not become a food faddist, there is no need to take vitamin or mineral supplements unless you have been ill.

Carbohydrates: the powerhouse of the diet and one area where vegetarians can't fail. Nearly all the basics in a vegetarian diet contain large amounts of carbohydrates and that vital other ingredient, dietary fibre, needed for a healthy digestive and immune system.

JUST THE TWO OF US
or Life Before Children ('BC') and Occasionally After

I'm sure for many of us, life before children seems a somewhat distant memory, with strange habits such as 'lying in bed in the morning', 'staying awake until well past midnight', and even more outrageously 'not having to cook', forming the bedrock of existence.

Dinner parties, of course, are as much part and parcel of family life after children as they were 'BC', although generally by the time you and your partner have had a couple of children these nocturnal home entertainments have become rather slick affairs. It is here that you must be careful – all too often couples can become too well organized. There is nothing worse than going to dinner with the 'Lasagne People' or the 'Curry Couple', who, despite being kind and generous never seem to realize that every time you go to eat there, that magical element of surprise is always missing. More importantly your guests might not particularly like lasagne or curry! Of course there's always the clever host who records all details of a dinner party – who came to dinner and what the menu was – thus managing to repeat favourite dishes but not always for the same friends.

This chapter, more than any other in the book, is for 'Us' whether 'BC' or not. Of course if you have children they are bound to want some the next day, but at least your efforts will not have been wasted if they don't like it.

For those special, relaxed evenings, here are some examples of dinner party menus. The recipes are mouth-watering, most of them can be prepared in advance and they can also be used for day time gatherings – after all, without the children to consider, afternoons and evenings just roll into one.

DINNER PARTY ONE
serves four

This is an interesting menu, and most of the recipes can be prepared in advance. The Walnut and Cheese Pâté used to be a great favourite at the restaurant, and the Double Chocolate, Nut and Raisin Delight... well, it's delicious.

Walnut and Cream Cheese Pâté with Warm Olive Bread

Normandy Galettes with Country Cider Sauce
Noodles with Spinach
Roasted Red Peppers and Onions

Double Chocolate, Nut and Raisin Delight

DINNER PARTY TWO
serves four

Burritos as a main course make for an informal atmosphere over the table. Virtually anything goes with a burrito, so they are ideal for using leftover cooked beans or vegetables. The Raspberry Cream Pots provide a light finish.

Chilli Bean Soup with Nachos

Burritos with Fire Sauce and Salsa
Stir-fried Broccoli and Cashews
Herby Green Salad

Raspberry Cream Pots

DINNER PARTY THREE
serves four

This dinner party menu has a distinctly oriental slant to it. I enjoy cooking oriental food – primarily I suppose because it's 95% preparation and only 5% cooking in most cases. The first cook I worked with at 'Food For Thought' was Siraporn from Thailand. Her thoughts on cooking have stayed with me ever since: keep food fresh and the flavours simple.

Thai Satay Soup

Shiitake and Tempeh Teriyaki Skewers with Dipping Sauce
Szechuan Braised Peppers
Yellow Chinese Rice

Tropical Caramel Cream

DINNER PARTY FOUR
serves four

This dinner party has a distinctly Italian flavour. My love affair with warm salads continues. The menu combines two seemingly contrary techniques – Grilled Salad and Roasted Vegetable Lasagne. Both ideas work extremely well and will certainly surprise your guests.

Grilled Salad with Mustard and Sherry Vinaigrette

Milanese Roasted Vegetable Lasagne
Swiss Chard with Lime
Mushroom Crostini

Strawberry and Fresh Fig Brûlée

Overleaf Left - WALNUT AND CREAM CHEESE PÂTÉ WITH WARM OLIVE BREAD *Right* - NORMANDY GALETTES WITH COUNTRY CIDER SAUCE, NOODLES WITH SPINACH, ROASTED RED PEPPERS AND ONIONS.

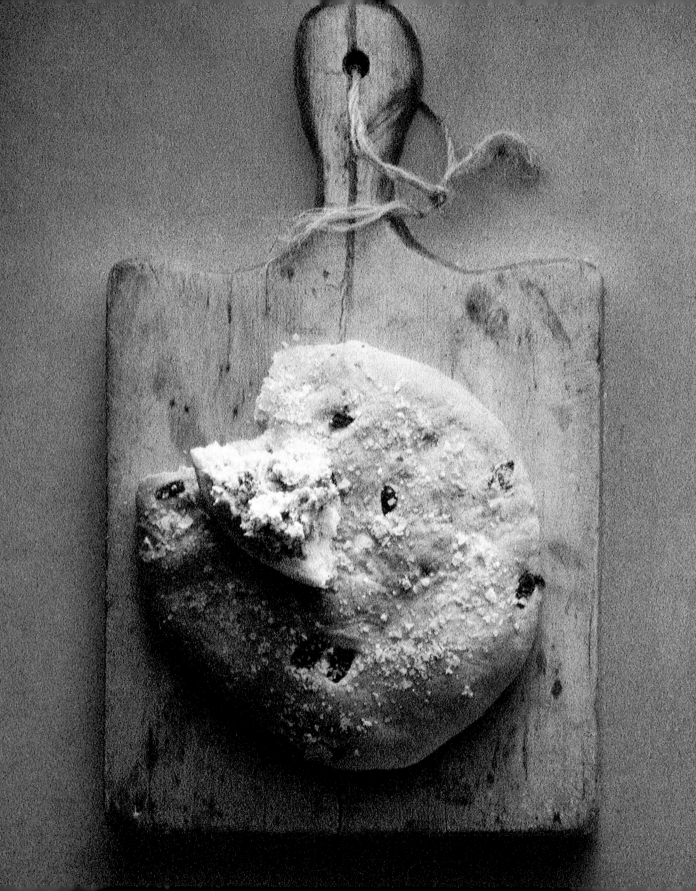

Walnut and Cream Cheese Pâté

50 g (2 oz) unsalted butter

4 shallots or small onions, finely chopped

1 teaspoon paprika

2 garlic cloves, crushed

1 teaspoon snipped fresh chives

400 g (13 oz) cottage cheese

50 ml (2 fl oz) soured cream

250 g (8 oz) ricotta cheese

250 g (8 oz) walnuts, lightly toasted and chopped

2 teaspoons Dijon mustard

2 teaspoons lemon juice

250 g (8 oz) vegetarian mature Cheddar cheese, grated

fine sea salt and freshly ground black pepper

TO DECORATE:

125 g (4 oz) cream cheese

2 spring onions, finely chopped

50 g (2 oz) walnut pieces, toasted

25 g (1 oz) black olives, pitted

This pâté was a great favourite at the restaurant. Uncannily meaty, it should be frozen if you want to keep it for more than a week.

1 Use 15 g (½ oz) of the butter to grease a 1 kg (2 lb) loaf tin. In a small, heavy saucepan melt the rest of the butter and sauté the shallots until beginning to soften.

2 In a bowl or food processor beat the rest of the ingredients together then fold in the shallots. Spoon the mixture into the greased loaf tin, spreading it evenly. Place in a preheated oven, 160°C (325°F), Gas Mark 3, for 1 hour.

3 Remove the pâté from the oven and allow to cool. When cool the pâté must be refrigerated for a further 3 hours before it can be turned out of its tin on to a plate.

4 To decorate, beat the cream cheese with the spring onions in a small bowl and season with salt and pepper to taste. Spread it over the pâté and decorate with walnuts and olives.

5 To serve, cut the pâté into slices and serve with a salad garnish, together with your favourite hot or toasted bread.

Olive Bread

300 g (10 oz) unbleached strong white flour

1 heaped teaspoon fine sea salt

20 g (¾ oz) fresh yeast, or ½ teaspoon
 active dried yeast

175 ml (6 fl oz) warm water

½ teaspoon brown demerara sugar

1 tablespoon extra virgin olive oil

10 black olives, pitted

3 garlic cloves, crushed (optional)

1 tablespoon chopped fresh rosemary, thyme or
 sage (optional)

2 tablespoons chopped sun-dried tomatoes and/or
 green olives (optional)

½ tablespoon coarse sea salt

extra virgin olive oil, for drizzling

Olive bread is a delicious, moist, flat bread originally made in the hearths of Italian kitchens. It is commonly known as Focaccia or Schiacciata. Enriched with olive oil Focaccia will re-heat success-fully and is a superb accompaniment to pâtés, soups and cheese.

1 Place the flour in a large bowl and mix in the fine sea salt. Crumble the fresh yeast into some of the warm water with the sugar in a jug or bowl, cover and allow to stand for 10 minutes until it starts to froth.

2 Make a well in the flour, add the yeast mixture and the olive oil and start to knead the dough, adding more water if necessary. The dough must be soft so make it on the sticky side. Place it in a clean, warm, lightly oiled bowl and cover with a damp tea towel. Leave to stand in a warm draught-free place until doubled in bulk, about 30-40 minutes.

3 Remove the dough from the bowl and place on a clean, lightly floured work surface. Knead in the olives and any of the other ingredients – garlic, herbs, sun-dried tomatoes or green olives – you wish to include. As you knead the dough, shape it into a ball. Place the ball of dough on a greased baking sheet then spread it out with your fingers to form a round 30 cm (12 inches) in diameter and 1 cm (½ inch) thick. Brush the surface with a little water and sprinkle with the coarse sea salt. Let it rise a second time in a warm place until it has doubled in size, then bake on the middle shelf of a preheated oven, 220°C (425°F), Gas Mark 7, for about 20 minutes.

4 Remove from the oven and drizzle with extra virgin olive oil and sprinkle on more coarse sea salt, if liked. Focaccia is best eaten warm and may easily be reheated in a hot oven for 5-10 minutes.

Normandy Galettes

1 tablespoon sunflower oil

1 onion, finely chopped

3 garlic cloves, crushed

1 tablespoon chopped fresh thyme

125 g (4 oz) celery, finely diced

125 g (4 oz) celeriac, grated

375 g (12 oz) courgettes, grated

1 tablespoon shoyu

1 tablespoon wholegrain mustard

750 ml (1¼ pints) hot water, or half water and half
   white wine

250 g (8 oz) granary breadcrumbs

300 g (10 oz) cooked brown rice

2 free range eggs, beaten (optional)

COATING:

2 free range eggs, beaten

125 g (4 oz) granary breadcrumbs

50 g (2 oz) sesame seeds or regular oats

fine sea salt and freshly ground black pepper

oil, for shallow-frying

'Galette' is a generic term for almost anything round, flat, edible and shallow-fried. They are usually made out of potatoes or grains but can also resemble robust pancakes.

1 Heat the oil in a frying pan. Add the onion, garlic and thyme and cook until the onion begins to soften. Add the celery, celeriac and courgettes and continue to cook for another 8 minutes.

2 Stir in the shoyu and mustard. Add the water, or water and wine, and bring to the boil, simmer for 3 minutes then remove from the heat.

3 Fold in the breadcrumbs, rice and beaten egg, if using, and mix to a smooth consistency. Divide the mixture into 8 and roll into balls. With lightly floured hands flatten each ball to form a galette about 1 cm (½ inch) thick. Chill them for several hours or, if time permits, overnight, before moving on to the next stage.

4 For the coating, place the beaten egg in a shallow saucer. Mix together the breadcrumbs, sesame seeds or oats and seasoning and place in another saucer. Dip each galette in the beaten egg then dip in the breadcrumb mixture, coating thoroughly.

5 Shallow-fry the galettes in hot oil in a large frying pan until they are golden brown all over, about 5 minutes on each side. Serve hot with Country Cider Sauce (see page 22).

Country Cider Sauce

25 g (1 oz) butter

4 shallots, finely chopped

2½ tablespoons unbleached plain white flour

900 ml (1½ pints) dry cider

150 ml (¼ pint) single cream

squeeze of lemon

50 g (1 oz) unsalted butter, chilled (optional)

fine sea salt and freshly ground black pepper

1 Melt the butter in a saucepan. Add the shallots and cook gently until beginning to soften. Stir in the flour and cook for 1 minute. Add the cider gradually, stirring all the time. Boil rapidly until the sauce thickens then leave over a low heat to simmer.

2 Place the cream in a separate saucepan, heat gently to reduce by half, then gradually add the cider sauce.

3 Add a few drops of lemon juice, and, if you are not serving the sauce immediately, a few cubes of chilled unsalted butter. Adjust the seasoning to taste.

Noodles with Spinach

500 g (1 lb) spinach, stalks removed

375 g (12 oz) dried tagliatelle

50 g (2 oz) unsalted butter

1 onion, thinly sliced

3 garlic cloves, crushed

pinch of freshly grated nutmeg

1 tablespoon lightly toasted breadcrumbs

fine sea salt and freshly ground black pepper

I love noodles with spinach – any noodles will do and the spinach has to be fresh. They make a particularly pleasant accompaniment to anything that has been pan-fried – try them and you will be converted too! Buy firm fresh leaves which are bright in colour and crisp in texture.

1 Wash the spinach in plenty of cold water being careful not to leave it immersed which will make it go soggy. Just dip it in and out until you feel that it is clean.

2 Put a large saucepan of water on to boil and cook the pasta according to the packet instructions. (The water should have a gently rolling boil when the pasta is added.)

3 Melt the butter in a deep saucepan, add the onion and sauté gently for 5-6 minutes. Add the garlic and spinach and cook for a further 4-5 minutes until the spinach is just cooked. Season to taste with nutmeg, salt and pepper.

4 When the pasta is cooked drain it thoroughly and fold into the spinach. Tip the pasta and spinach into a large serving dish and sprinkle with the lightly toasted breadcrumbs. Serve immediately.

Roasted Red Peppers and Onions

4 red peppers, cored, deseeded and quartered

4 small onions, peeled and halved

1 tablespoon extra virgin olive oil

1 teaspoon dried thyme

fine sea salt and freshly ground black pepper

This side dish is so simple that you'll feel guilty that you haven't done any real work. The sad thing is that the peppers tend to disappear not only in the oven but as soon as they are served, so I suggest making a bit more than would normally seem necessary as there are never, ever, leftover roasted red peppers!

1 Brush a roasting tin with a little of the olive oil. Place the vegetables in the tin then brush them with the remaining olive oil. Sprinkle with thyme, season and place in a preheated oven, 200°C (400°F), Gas Mark 6, for 20-30 minutes or until well roasted and soft.

2 Remove from the oven, transfer to a dish and serve. (I do not recommend removing the skins unless they are black.)

Double Chocolate, Nut and Raisin Delight

3 tablespoons brandy

3 tablespoons Cointreau or Triplesec

1 tablespoon Amaretto

1 tablespoon strong black coffee

375 g (12 oz) amaretti sponges

450 ml (¾ pint) double cream

125 g (4 oz) icing sugar

125 g (4 oz) white chocolate, broken into pieces

50 g (2 oz) Belgian dark chocolate, broken into pieces

50 g (2 oz) nibbed almonds, toasted

50 g (2 oz) nibbed hazelnuts, toasted

50 g (2 oz) plump black raisins (soaked in
   brandy, if liked)

Here's a dessert that will certainly cause a stir – definitely one to save for the adults. You will need a 1.5 litre (2½ pint) pudding basin lined with damp muslin.

I suggest using amaretti sponges for the flavour if possible, but ordinary sponge fingers are fine, too.

1 Line a 1.5 litre (2½ pint) pudding basin with damp muslin.

2 Mix the liqueurs and coffee together in a small bowl.

3 Line the amaretti sponges around the insides of the basin, on top of the muslin, making sure that they fit snugly – retain enough sponges for the top of the pudding. Soak the sponges in two-thirds of the liqueur mixture, setting the remaining third aside.

4 Whip the double cream with the icing sugar until soft peaks form and divide into 2 separate bowls.

5 Place the white chocolate in a small heatproof bowl and place over a saucepan of gently simmering water. When melted and cooled, whisk the chocolate into the cream in one of the bowls until the mixture is very firm. Repeat for the dark chocolate.

6 Fold the nuts into the white chocolate mousse and then spread the mixture on to the insides of the sponges lining the basin. Add the raisins to the dark chocolate mousse and pour this mixture into the centre of the pudding.

7 Dip the remaining sponges into the reserved liqueur mixture and place on top of the pudding. Cover with the muslin, then place a saucer or small plate on top. Weight down and refrigerate for at least 12 hours.

8 To serve, remove the weight and saucer or plate. Turn the pudding out on to a serving plate, and remove the muslin.

Chilli Bean Soup with Nachos

2 tablespoons extra virgin olive oil

1 red onion, chopped

3 garlic cloves, crushed

1 teaspoon ground cumin

1 fresh red chilli, deseeded and chopped

1 teaspoon dried basil

1 teaspoon dried oregano

½ tablespoon lime or lemon juice

½ tablespoon demerara sugar

3 tablespoons tomato purée

2 x 425 g (14 oz) cans black kidney beans

1 tablespoon vegetarian Worcestershire sauce

1 tablespoon shoyu

1.2 litres (2 pints) vegetable stock

TOPPING:

2 x 20 cm (8 inch) corn tortillas, or ready-made
  corn chips

oil, for frying

50 g (2 oz) vegetarian mature Cheddar cheese, grated

crème fraîche, to serve (optional)

This hearty soup could easily turn into a main course if you're not careful. In addition to nachos try adding soured cream, guacamole, a salsa or even just chopped fresh coriander. The soup is best made the day before eating it.

1 Heat the oil in a large heavy saucepan or casserole dish, add the onion, garlic, spices, chilli and herbs and sauté together gently for 6 minutes. Add the remaining ingredients and bring to the boil. Then simmer for 25-30 minutes.

2 Remove half of the soup and purée it before returning it to the rest of the soup in the pan. (This is best done the day before.)

3 Cut each corn tortilla, if using, into 8 wedges and fry in a little oil until crisp. Alternatively, use ready-made corn chips.

4 To serve, pour the soup into ovenproof bowls. Top with corn chips and cheese, place under the grill for a few minutes until the cheese is bubbling and golden. Serve with crème fraîche, if liked.

Burritos with Fire Sauce and Salsa

8 x 20 cm (8 inch) flour tortillas (see page 128)

150 ml (¼ pint) soured cream

1 tablespoon chopped fresh chives or mint

125 g (4 oz) mozzarella cheese, grated (optional)

25 g (1 oz) freshly grated Parmesan cheese (optional)

fine sea salt and freshly ground black pepper

BURRITOS FILLING:

2 tablespoons olive oil

1 onion, finely chopped

1 small aubergine, cut into 1 cm (½ inch) cubes

1 red pepper, cored, deseeded and diced

175 g (6 oz) flat mushrooms, chopped

2 garlic cloves, crushed

50 g (2 oz) nibbed almonds, toasted

200 g (7 oz) can sweetcorn, drained

125 g (4 oz) vegetarian mature Cheddar cheese,
  grated (optional)

FIRE SAUCE:

1 tablespoon olive oil

1 onion, finely chopped

3 garlic cloves, crushed

2 teaspoons ground cumin

2 teaspoons dried oregano

2 fresh red chillies (deseeded for a milder sauce)

¼ teaspoon ground coriander

175 ml (6 fl oz) red wine

2 tablespoons tomato purée

2 x 425 g (14 oz) cans chopped tomatoes

1 teaspoon orange rind

SALSA:

1 red pepper, cored, deseeded and halved

1 fresh jalapeno chilli, halved (deseeded
   for a milder sauce)

extra virgin olive oil, for brushing

2 ripe avocados

2 tablespoons lemon or lime juice

1 bunch of spring onions, white parts only, chopped

2 teaspoons chopped fresh coriander, to garnish

If it's not a really special occasion, Burritos are an ideal way of using up leftover cooked beans and vegetables – just about everything goes and like all good Mexican food you can bolt on as many extras as you feel happy with. Burritos are essentially anything wrapped up in a soft flour tortilla and baked.

For this recipe simply warm the tortillas through in a microwave to loosen them up if necessary – this will make rolling them easier. Don't re-cook them. The filling can be made a day in advance, and the Fire Sauce is best made the day before eating. Chilli sauces are very much a matter of personal taste so adjust the heat to your own preference.

The salsa is best made just before serving – everything can be prepared in advance except for the avocados.

1 To make the filling, heat the oil in a large saucepan or casserole dish. Add the onion and aubergine and cook gently for 5 minutes, stirring occasionally to prevent sticking or burning.

2 Stir in the red pepper, mushrooms and garlic. Cover and cook gently for 10 minutes before adding the almonds and sweetcorn. Season to taste.

3 Divide the mixture evenly between the 8 tortillas and top with cheese, if using, before rolling them up tightly into cylindrical shapes. Place in a lightly oiled baking dish.

4 For the fire sauce, heat the oil in a deep heavy saucepan. Add the onion, garlic, cumin, oregano, chillies and coriander. Cook until the onion begins to soften and darken in colour. Turn up the heat and add the red wine. Simmer until reduced by half. Stir in the tomato purée followed by the chopped tomatoes. Bring to the boil then simmer for at least 30 minutes and up to 3 hours. Turn off the heat, season to taste and stir in the orange rind.

5 Meanwhile, stir the soured cream and spoon into a serving dish or individual ramekins. Season with a little coarse ground black pepper and a little chopped chives or mint.

6 To make the salsa, brush the red pepper and the chilli with a little olive oil and roast in a preheated oven, 200°C (400°F), Gas Mark 6, for about 15-20 minutes, until the skins begin to blister. Remove from the oven and allow to cool before chopping into small dice.

7 Halve the avocados, remove the stones and scoop out the flesh into a mixing bowl. Immediately beat in the lemon or lime juice to delay discoloration. Combine all the ingredients with a fork (not in a blender). Place in a serving dish or individual ramekins and sprinkle with chopped coriander.

8 To assemble the burritos, pour the fire sauce around the burritos in their dish, trying to avoid splashing the tops. Sprinkle the tops with a little grated mozzarella and Parmesan, if using.

9 Bake in a preheated oven, 160°C (325°F), Gas Mark 3, until the cheese is melted, bubbling and brown, about 40 minutes.

10 Serve the burritos with the salsa and soured cream, preferably providing each guest with their own little ramekin of each.

Stir-fried Broccoli and Cashews

2 tablespoons oil

750 g (1½ lb) broccoli, cut into florets.

1 medium carrot, cut into julienne strips

2 garlic cloves, crushed

50 g (2 oz) cashew nuts

1 bunch spring onions, chopped

1 tablespoon shoyu

fine sea salt and freshly ground black pepper

Many vegetable dishes at dinner parties are for ease, precooked or preheated. Occasionally you're given something fresh, something that takes a little time and effort at the last moment, but also something that is appreciated.

1 Heat the oil in a heavy frying pan or wok. When the oil is very hot, add the broccoli and carrot and stir-fry for 3 minutes. Then add the garlic, cashews and spring onions and stir-fry for about 4 minutes. Add the shoyu and let it reduce by half. Season to taste, cover and steam for 5 minutes.

Note. This dish is very versatile - I have kept it fairly bland as it is accompanying some pretty hot stuff! Other additions would be ginger, sherry, chilli, spices and virtually any vegetable.

Herby Green Salad

1 gem lettuce

8 young spinach leaves

1 head of chicory

8 leaves of curly endive

8 leaves of rocket

1 tablespoon chopped fresh chervil

1 tablespoon chopped fresh mint

2 tablespoons torn basil leaves

1 tablespoon snipped fresh chives

DRESSING:

6 tablespoons extra virgin olive oil

4 tablespoons balsamic vinegar

fine sea salt and freshly ground black pepper

Giving recipes for salads always feels to me like telling someone how to make love. No doubt there are lots of tips that can be passed on. One tip, however, is to avoid using knives when preparing salad leaves.

1 Mix the leaves and herbs together in a large salad bowl. Combine the dressing ingredients and toss with the salad.

Raspberry Cream Pots

250 g (8 oz) raspberries

3 tablespoons demerara sugar

4 egg yolks

275 ml (9 fl oz) double cream

1½ tablespoons framboise or kirsch

soured cream or crème fraîche, to decorate

After such a substantial and fairly spicy meal a light fruity dessert is required. This one has the added advantage of being able to be prepared hours beforehand.

1 Reserve a few raspberries for decoration and place the rest in a liquidizer or food processor with the sugar and eggs. Blend together then rub through a sieve into a bowl. Stir in the cream and framboise or kirsch; then pour into 4 individual ramekins.

2 Place the ramekins in an ovenproof dish or roasting tin containing enough hot water to cover two-thirds of the depth of the ramekins. Place in a preheated oven, 140°C (275°F), Gas Mark 1, for at least 1 hour until the edges are set and the centres are slightly wobbly.

3 Allow the pots to cool, then chill for 6 hours.

4 To serve, top each ramekin with a dollop of soured cream or crème fraîche and the reserved raspberries.

Thai Satay Soup

1 stalk of lemon grass, roughly chopped

6 shallots, roughly chopped

4 garlic cloves, crushed

2.5 cm (1 inch) piece of fresh root ginger, finely chopped

½ teaspoon ground turmeric

½ teaspoon chilli powder

2 tablespoons lemon juice or tamarind sauce

2 tablespoons water

1 tablespoon sesame oil

1 litre (1¾ pints) vegetable stock

175 g (6 oz) dried medium egg noodles

425 g (14 oz) can coconut milk

250 g (8 oz) firm tofu, cut into 1 cm (½ inch) cubes

125 g (4 oz) bean sprouts

75 g (3 oz) Chinese black mushrooms, sliced

fine sea salt and freshly ground black pepper

Siraporn would certainly have approved of this soup. It has clean lines and a clear distinctive flavour. Don't be put off by the longish list of ingredients, it's easy.

1 Blend the first 6 ingredients together in a bowl with 1 tablespoon of the lemon juice or tamarind sauce and the water to form a paste. Heat the sesame oil in a large heavy saucepan. Stir into the paste, return this to the pan and cook for about 15 minutes. Add the vegetable stock, stir and bring to the boil then simmer for a further 15 minutes.

2 Meanwhile, in another saucepan, cook the noodles according to the packet instructions.

3 Strain the soup into a clean pan and add the coconut milk. Add the tofu, bean sprouts and mushrooms and simmer for 3 minutes.

4 Drain the cooked noodles and add to the soup with the rest of the lemon juice or tamarind sauce. Season to taste with salt and pepper and serve the soup piping hot.

Shiitake and Tempeh Teriyaki Skewers

500 g (1 lb) shiitake mushrooms

500 g (1 lb) tempeh, cut into 2.5 cm (1 inch) cubes

sunflower oil, for shallow-frying

1 tablespoon coriander leaves, to garnish

MARINADE:

125 ml (4 fl oz) mirin

50 ml (2 fl oz) shoyu

2 tablespoons sesame oil

2 tablespoons lemon juice

1 tablespoon ginger juice, or grated ginger

BATTER:

1 egg

250 ml (8 fl oz) ice-cold water

pinch of bicarbonate of soda

75 g (3 oz) unbleached plain white flour

fine sea salt and freshly ground black pepper

DIPPING SAUCE:

75 g (3 oz) light tahini (do not use dark, toasted tahini)

25 g (1 oz) cashew nut butter

50 g (2 oz) barley miso

175 ml (6 fl oz) marinade

2 garlic cloves, crushed

This recipe is a bit of a cheat on two counts, although they can be grilled the skewers are much better shallow-fried and I prefer to use the dipping sauce as a sploshing sauce. In other words I tend to pour it over the skewers to ensure even distribution. If you are a vegan leave out the Tempura batter or substitute it with a Pakora batter and deep-fry the skewers.

Soak the wooden skewers in water before use to prevent them from burning. You will need 12 skewers.

Overleaf Left- THAI SATAY SOUP *Right-* SHIITAKE AND TEMPEH TERIYAKI SKEWERS, SZECHUAN BRAISED PEPPERS, YELLOW CHINESE RICE.

1 Mix the marinade ingredients in a clean, plastic container. Add the mushrooms and tempeh and allow to marinate in a cool place for at least 3 hours or overnight.

2 Remove the mushrooms and the tempeh from the marinade with a slotted spoon and allow to drain thoroughly on a wire rack before threading alternately on to the skewers.

3 Whisk the batter ingredients together until frothy. Tempura batter should be very thin – if it is at all thick add a little more iced water. Do not overbeat the batter.

4 When ready to eat, simply dip the skewers in the batter and shallow-fry in hot sunflower oil. Keep warm in the oven.

5 The dipping sauce can be made as soon as the mushrooms and tempeh are removed from the marinade by simply stirring all the ingredients together until well combined.

Szechuan Braised Peppers

4 large red, yellow or green peppers, cored,
    deseeded and quartered

sesame oil, for brushing

a little vegetable oil, for oiling

½ quantity Teriyaki marinade (see Shiitake and
    Tempeh Teriyaki Skewers, page 27)

3 teaspoons brown sugar

6 spring onions, finely sliced

3 tablespoons chopped fresh coriander

1 teaspoon hot chilli sauce

25 g (1 oz) sesame seeds, toasted

fine sea salt

This is a very simple and tasty recipe that will add plenty of colour and flavour to any meal. Eaten with the Shiitake and Tempeh Teriyaki Skewers (see page 27) it also conveniently uses up the rest of the marinade. Obviously if you are not using the skewer recipe and cooking these peppers as an accompaniment to

another meal you'll have to make up about half the quantity of the marinade used for the skewers.

1 Lightly brush the quarters of pepper with the sesame oil and place them on a lightly oiled baking sheet in a preheated oven, 200°C (400°F), Gas Mark 6 and cook for about 30 minutes.

2 Meanwhile, mix the marinade with the rest of the ingredients, except the sesame seeds.

3 When the peppers are ready, cut into strips and toss in the dressing. Sprinkle with toasted sesame seeds and serve.

Yellow Chinese Rice

175 g (6 oz) Basmati rice

25 g (1 oz) Camargue Red rice

a few saffron threads

1 tablespoon water

5 cm (2 inch) piece of lemon grass

3-4 tablespoons sesame oil

50 g (2 oz) cashew nuts

1 large onion, shredded

2 garlic cloves, crushed

1 fresh green chilli, finely sliced

50 g (2 oz) bamboo shoots

25 g (1 oz) red pickled ginger

125 g (4 oz) green beans or sugar snaps,
    blanched thoroughly

Here's a delicious rice recipe that would make a meal on its own. Chinese and Japanese cooks tend to use short- or medium-grained rice to accompany their savoury dishes but if you prefer, use a long-grain rice like Basmati. Red rice from the Camargue in France is a tasty addition and contrasts well with the yellow colour which is a feature of the saffron rice. If you can't get saffron use 1½ teaspoons turmeric instead - it will still give a good yellow colouring.

1 Thoroughly wash both lots of rice separately under cold running water and then drain well. Soak the saffron threads in the mea-

sured water for about 10-15 minutes and then set aside.

2 Cook the Basmati rice in a large saucepan of water with the saffron and the lemon grass for about 10-15 minutes until just tender. Drain well and cool. Cook the red rice separately in boiling water until tender.

3 Heat 2 tablespoons of sesame oil in a large heavy frying pan. Add the cashews and fry until golden. Remove with a slotted spoon and set aside. Add the shredded onion, garlic and chilli and cook for about 10 minutes over a reasonably high heat, stirring frequently to prevent burning. Pour in the rest of the sesame oil, heat then stir in the remaining ingredients and both quantities of the rice, mixing well.

4 If you're short of time for serving, the rice can be covered with foil and kept warm in the oven. Alternatively, cook it earlier in the day and re-heat it in the microwave, before combining with the other ingredients.

5 Garnish the rice with the fried cashews and serve immediately. This dish is goes extremely well the Szechuan Braised Peppers and Shiitake and Tempeh Teriyaki Skewers (see pages 27-30).

Tropical Caramel Cream

1 ripe banana, thickly sliced

1 small ripe pineapple, cut into
   1 cm (½ inch) cubes

1 small Charentais melon, cut into
   1 cm (½ inch) cubes

2 passion fruit, halved

2 tablespoons Pineau des Charentes

2 tablespoons freshly squeezed orange juice

150 ml (¼ pint) double cream

150 ml (¼ pint) Greek yogurt

50 g (2 oz) demerara sugar

1 tablespoon water

After a fairly taxing starter and main course it makes sense to have a simple sweet. If the rest of the food has been hot and spicy the ideal dessert will be cool, comforting and cleansing like this one. This dish is best served in large individual glasses or glass dessert bowls.

1 Divide the prepared fruit between 4 glass dessert bowls. Mix the Pineau des Charentes and orange juice together and pour over the fruit. (If preferred, substitute 1 tablespoon of rum for the aperitif and use 3 tablespoons of orange juice.)

2 Whip the cream until soft peaks form and fold in the Greek yogurt. Spoon this mixture generously over the fruit.

3 Gently heat the sugar with the water in a small heavy saucepan until the sugar has dissolved. Boil rapidly until the syrup is golden. Set aside to darken in colour.

4 Oil a large sheet of foil and pour the syrup over it in small and irregular shapes. Allow to cool. Peel off the caramel pieces and stick into the cream when you are ready to serve.

Milanese Roasted Vegetable Lasagne

12 sheets of lasagne, precooked in boiling water, then
  drained and cooled

sliced tomatoes, to garnish

MILANESE TOMATO SAUCE:

1½ tablespoons olive oil

1 onion, chopped

4 garlic cloves, crushed

1 green pepper, cored, deseeded and diced

125 g (4 oz) field mushrooms (porcini if possible),
  chopped

8 basil leaves, torn into pieces

2 teaspoons dried oregano

1 bay leaf

175 g (6 fl oz) full-bodied red wine

2 tablespoons tomato purée

2 x 425 g (14 oz) cans chopped tomatoes

250 g (8 oz) fresh tomatoes, skinned, deseeded
  and chopped

FILLING:

2 tablespoons extra virgin olive oil

1 large aubergine, quartered

2 large courgettes, quartered

1 large red pepper, cored, deseeded and quartered

1 large yellow pepper cored, deseeded and quartered

1 fennel bulb, quartered

4 shallots or small onions, halved

1 tablespoon dried thyme or similar herb

fine sea salt and freshly ground black pepper

CHEESE SAUCE:

750 ml (1¼ pints) milk

75 g (3 oz) butter

50 g (2 oz) unbleached plain white flour

1 egg yolk (optional)

50 g (2 oz) Gorgonzola, dolcelatte or Stilton
  cheese, grated

50 g (2 oz) mature vegetarian Cheddar cheese, grated

50 g (2 oz) mozzarella cheese, grated

½ teaspoon cayenne pepper

2 tablespoons soured cream (optional)

fine sea salt and freshly ground black pepper

*In recent years I seem to be increasingly roasting or grilling veg-
etables basted with olive oil, and perhaps seasoned or sprinkled
with herbs. For a start, I love the flavour that develops; secondly
the texture of the vegetables changes wonderfully and, thirdly the
individual vegetables seem to retain more of their own identity
than if they had been stir-fried together. My favourite vegetables
for roasting, apart from the traditional ones of course, are
aubergines, peppers, courgettes, tomatoes, onions, fennel, garlic
and shallots. The technique is very simple and well worth experimenting with.*

*All sorts of lasagne are available these days. If you can't get
or make fresh lasagne, buy the type that requires boiling. 'No precook' lasagne, is a bit of a risk as it tends to absorb water from
your sauce making the dish a little dry. You can compensate by
making runnier sauces but I find this a bit hit and miss. Try and
make the Tomato Sauce the day before as it improves with age.*

1 Make the tomato sauce well in advance. Heat the oil in a pan,
sauté the onion until soft then add the rest of the vegetables and
herbs and cook for a further 5 minutes. Add the wine and cook
gently to reduce by half. Stir in the tomato purée quickly followed
by the canned and fresh tomatoes. Bring to the boil then gently
simmer for at least 1 hour (2 hours would be better). Set the sauce
aside to cool, then refrigerate.

2 The filling is simple to make. Brush a baking sheet with olive oil;
brush each piece of vegetable with oil and arrange on the baking
sheet. Season with dried herbs, salt and pepper. Roast in a preheated oven, 200°C (400°F), Gas Mark 6, until cooked, about
40-60 minutes. Set aside to cool. When cool you may wish to cut
the vegetables further – I prefer them chunky myself.

3 Make the cheese sauce by warming the milk in a large heavy saucepan. Melt the butter in another saucepan, add the flour and cook for a few minutes without letting it colour. Then gradually add the warmed milk, stirring constantly to keep the mixture smooth. When all the milk has been added let the sauce simmer very gently for about 10 minutes. Stir in the egg yolk, if using, cheeses and seasoning and remove from the heat. Add the soured cream and adjust the seasoning, if necessary.

4 To assemble the lasagne, brush the bottom of a 3 litre (5 pint) ovenproof dish generously with olive oil. Place 4 sheets of lasagne on the bottom of the dish and top with half of the tomato sauce, half of the roasted vegetables and one-third of the cheese sauce. Top this with 4 more sheets of lasagne and repeat the process until you have one-third of the cheese sauce left, with which to top the remaining layer of lasagne. Garnish with the tomato slices.

5 Place in a preheated oven, 180°C (350°F), Gas Mark 4 and bake for about 45-55 minutes, or until the top is golden. Allow the lasagne to stand for 10 minutes before serving with the grilled salad and Swiss chard .

Grilled Salad with Mustard and Sherry Vinaigrette

1 head of chicory, pulled apart

12 leaves of rocket, or 1 head of gem lettuce

175 g (6 oz) fresh sun-ripened tomatoes, skinned, deseeded and diced

50 g (2 oz) sun-dried tomatoes, chopped

2 radicchio, cut into 8 wedges

50 g (2 oz) walnut pieces

125 g (4 oz) goats' cheese, crumbled, or
   50 g (2 oz) freshly grated Parmesan cheese
   (both optional)

fine sea salt and freshly ground black pepper

VINAIGRETTE:

3 garlic cloves, crushed

1 tablespoon wholegrain mustard

2 tablespoons sherry vinegar

6 tablespoons extra virgin olive oil

1 tablespoon chopped fresh parsley

1 tablespoon snipped fresh chives

1 teaspoon chopped fresh tarragon

fine sea salt and freshly ground black pepper

If you are short of time and ingredients for this salad, the radicchio grilled on its own with the vinaigrette is a wonderful treat.

1 Make the vinaigrette dressing well in advance, to allow the flavours to mingle, by combining the ingredients thoroughly.

2 Mix together the chicory, rocket or lettuce and tomatoes in a salad bowl.

3 Toss the radicchio in half of the vinaigrette dressing and pop it under a preheated grill with the walnuts, until it is browning around the edges.

4 Add to the rest of the salad and sprinkle with the remaining vinaigrette and the cheese. Season to taste and serve.

Swiss Chard with Lime

875 g (1¾ lb) Swiss chard, or 625 g (1¼ lb) fresh spinach

juice of 1 fresh lime

4 tablespoons extra virgin olive oil

fine sea salt and freshly ground black pepper

Quick and simple, this is a delicious accompaniment to something rich like the Roasted Vegetable Lasagne. Much as I love fresh spinach, given the choice I would always choose chard. For some reason it is usually fresher and more flavoursome than spinach.

Remove the large central spine with a sharp knife and cook it separately or save it for a stir-fry the next day.

1 Prepare the chard or spinach. Tear the larger leaves apart and wash thoroughly. Chard leaves can be a bit gritty but, unlike spinach, will not wilt so readily in water.

2 Mix the lime juice with 3 tablespoons of olive oil and season with salt and pepper.

3 In a saucepan heat the remaining olive oil, add the chard and stir. Cover and allow to cook for 5 minutes over a medium heat, then remove the lid. The chard should be almost cooked, give it a stir and replace the lid for 1 minute more.

4 Just before serving, stir in the lime and oil, mixing well.

Mushroom Crostini

8 tablespoons extra virgin olive oil

1 baguette, about 250 g (8 oz), cut diagonally into
   about 16 slices

2 tablespoons chopped fresh coriander

3 garlic cloves, crushed

50 g (2 oz) unsalted butter

175 g (6 oz) fresh ceps or cup mushrooms

50 ml (2 fl oz) dry white wine

25 g (1 oz) freshly grated vegetarian Parmesan
   cheese (optional)

fine sea salt and freshly ground black pepper

This is a good alternative to the more mundane garlic bread. If you can get them, use fresh ceps instead of, or as well as the fresh mushrooms. They are a delicious topping for crostini.

1 Use 6 tablespoons of the olive oil for brushing: brush a baking sheet with the oil and brush both sides of each baguette slice with olive oil. Arrange the slices on the baking sheet and place under a preheated grill. Brown both sides carefully – try not to overcook them, as they burn easily. Remove and cool.

2 Mix the coriander and garlic. Melt the butter and the remaining 2 tablespoons of olive oil in a frying pan. Add the mushrooms and sauté for 3 minutes. Add the wine and cook gently to reduce it by half. Lower the heat and stir in the chopped coriander, garlic

and season. Continue to cook gently for about 2 minutes more.

3 Remove from the heat, allow to cool and chop the mushrooms finely. Stir in Parmesan, if using, and set aside until ready to use.

5 Crostini are good served cold but even better warmed. Spoon some of the mushroom mixture on to each slice, then heat in the oven until the Parmesan has melted. Serve immediately.

Strawberry and Fresh Fig Brûlée

125 g (4 oz) very sound, ripe figs, sliced

125 g (4 oz) strawberries, halved, or whole,
   wild strawberries

1 vanilla pod, split lengthways

150 ml (¼ pint) double cream

150 ml (¼ pint) crème fraîche

4 egg yolks (size 4)

1 tablespoon fructose (fruit sugar)

demerara sugar, for sprinkling

After a substantial main course a light and fruity dessert is required. This variation of an old standard is always popular, so it's probably best to double the recipe and make 8 servings. Only use figs if they are perfectly ripe – if you can't get ripe figs use blackberries, blueberries or passion fruit.

1 Pile the fruit into and around the edges of 4 ramekin dishes. Place the vanilla pod in a pan. Stir in the two creams and heat to just below boiling point. Remove the pod.

2 Beat the egg yolks and fructose together in a pan then gradually beat in the hot vanilla cream. Heat gently until the sauce has thickened. Pour the custard over the fruit in the ramekins and set aside to cool. When cool, chill for 2-3 hours until set.

3 Sprinkle the puddings with a little demerara and grill under a preheated hot grill. The sugar should caramelize and when allowed to cool, forms a hard protective coating to the top of the custard cream. Serve cold.

AND BABY MAKES THREE

Cooking is an act of love and caring. Some believe that the 'kiss' – seemingly only associated with humans – originated as an expression of love. In the act of weaning their children, early female *Homosapiens* passed masticated food from their mouths directly into their children's mouths. There were many benefits attributed to this technique. Not only did the children start eating solids in a semi-liquid form, but also the food was much easier and safer to digest because it was mixed with the mother's saliva – a natural disinfectant and digestive. As the children grew older, feeding and then hunting and gathering food for themselves, this tender act was outgrown. Nowadays we have the food processor, the sieve and the hand-blender instead (I wonder what future anthropologists will make of them!). The 'kiss' does remain, however, the touching of two people's lips as the ultimate expression of human love, caring and kindness.

Before I go any further I feel that I should explain my qualifications in this subject. I am the father of three children – Daisy, twelve, Hamish, nine, and Mollie, three years old. Not unnaturally, all three have been brought up on a vegetarian diet, simply because their mother, Kate, is a vegetarian. Later in life they can make their own decisions but right now they eat what we eat at home, which is vegetarian food. I might add that Daisy, Hamish and Mollie are all of average height and intelligence. They have never suffered from anything more than the common cold; they don't suffer from flatulence; they look lovely, healthy and vibrant and they are all keen on sport. What is more they have never really had any health additives apart from those extra vitamins which mysteriously appear in cereal packets. In fact Hamish and Mollie have both been sick, related to food, once in their lives. Modern food pundits would expect our children to be sullen, thick, pale, physical wrecks, racked with lethargy and not nice to be in a confined space with. I am going to make a rather sensational statement now – it is not in my nature but I'm going to do it all the same: I think that all healthy women, during pregnancy and while breastfeeding, should be vegetarian and, equally, babies should be weaned on to pure vegetarian food, ideally organic – foods that have as few chemicals in or on them as possible. Why? Because it seems to me that the common problems associated with pregnancy and feeding after birth are diet or health related. Smoking, should be taboo but there's nothing much wrong with the odd glass of wine in the later stages – as a morale booster it could also be very beneficial. A good well-balanced vegetarian (not vegan) diet is what most babies should be made from. Daisy, Hamish and Mollie are, I believe, the best evidence of this. Meat is an outdated form of protein that is over-farmed and overpriced and if you want to be overweight, too, then carry on eating it – especially when you are pregnant.

It's all simple really, you are what you eat. In this chapter we will be looking at the four phases of feeding a baby. Firstly, during pregnancy before the baby is born; then the first 6 months when he or she will be primarily breast- or formula-fed. Then 6-12 months when more and more solids will be introduced and lastly from 12 months onwards when effectively the baby will be wanting to share in family meals.

DURING PREGNANCY

So, you're pregnant. I'm afraid I cannot speak from experience so these are the thoughts of my wife, Kate.

Everyone is different so it's best to speak broadly. The biggest misconception is to assume that because you are only just pregnant that somehow the effect on your body is less than when you're about to give birth. If anything, the reverse is true. The moment you conceive, your whole body starts to change. Even though the foetus is still microscopic it has a huge effect on you. Often the first change you experience is in your feelings towards food – for some women the mere thought of food makes them feel queasy. When I see relevant books on the subject recommending foods such as liver, kidney, oily fish, kippers and smoked fish, I wonder if the authors have ever been pregnant themselves or, at least known anyone who has experienced pregnancy. No doubt at the beginning of your pregnancy you will be happiest with plain foods but as your pregnancy develops you may start to desire strange combinations. Towards the end you eat only what you can squeeze into your distended stomach and drink what your flattened bladder allows.

As a healthy vegetarian there is absolutely no problem in obtaining all of the goodness you need to develop a healthy baby, but some foods must definitely be avoided. These include raw or undercooked eggs which may result in salmonella poisoning, and soft cheeses that are at risk from contamination by *listeria*. Generally though vegetarians do not have as many problems with 'risky' food as those who eat meat and fish. Too much fat will be a problem whether you are pregnant or not, but once again vegetarians tend to benefit here.

During an average week you will want to eat meals that include eggs, milk, cheese (mild vegetarian Cheddar at first), yogurt, fromage frais, seeds, pasta, cereals, beans, pulses, fresh vegetables, fresh fruit, nuts and cold-pressed oils. Fresh fruit will be a constant source of refreshment to your tastebuds and, of course, are excellent providers of Vitamin C. Do wash all fresh fruit and vegetables thoroughly before use, though, because any residual chemical sprays will go straight into your baby. Alternatively, buy good-quality organic produce.

Funnily enough, as you and your baby grow you will get over the initial shock to your body and despite the constant changing in your dimensions, things will seem more normal. As you become adjusted to your new state so your tastebuds will return, sometimes with a vengeance. From about 3-7 months your eating habits will return to somewhere near normal, with perhaps an extra couple of nutritious snacks fitted in here and there. You might also find that you cannot eat a meal late in the evening as your body takes longer to digest food, so rich food at a dinner party where the meal begins at 9.30 or 10 pm is not to be encouraged. It is of course important for the baby that you steadily increase your weight by at least 9-10 kg (18-20 lb) during the course of the pregnancy.

THE EARLY MONTHS

Here is a plain and wholesome menu to comfort you in those early and perhaps nauseous months of pregnancy. Use it as a dinner party or select component parts for meals on their own.

Serves 4

Creamy Onion and Thyme Flan

Pasta Panzanella

Spring Salad

Strawberry and Banana Chocolate Truffle Pavlova

Date and Nut Loaf

Creamy Onion and Thyme Flan

PASTRY:

75 g (3 oz) organic wholewheat flour

75 g (3 oz) unbleached plain white flour

2 teaspoons chopped fresh thyme

75 g (3 oz) unsalted butter

2-3 tablespoons ice-cold water

FILLING:

2 Spanish onions, quartered

1 red pepper, cored, deseeded and quartered

1 tablespoon extra virgin olive oil

3 free-range egg yolks

150 ml (¼ pint) single cream

150 ml (¼ pint) full-fat milk

½ teaspoon freshly grated nutmeg

75 g (3 oz) Gruyère cheese, grated

fine sea salt and freshly ground black pepper

sprigs of thyme, to garnish

Flans are, what real men don't eat! A good flan is delicious hot or cold and ideal as a starter.

1 Mix the flours and the thyme in a cold bowl. Rub in the butter with the fingertips until the mixture resembles fine breadcrumbs. Add enough of the cold water to mix to a smooth dough. Knead briefly before allowing the dough to chill for 30-60 minutes before rolling out.

2 Roll out the dough on a lightly floured surface and use to line a well-oiled 23 cm (9 inch) flan tin. If possible, freeze the flan case at this stage – frozen flan cases can be cooked from frozen without the use of baking beans. If you don't have time for this, line the flan case with greaseproof paper and half fill it with ceramic beans. Bake for 10 minutes in a preheated oven, 200°C (400°F), Gas Mark 6. Remove the beans and cook for a further 5 minutes. If baking the flan case blind from frozen, simply place it straight from the freezer into the oven and cook for 10 minutes.

3 Meanwhile, brush the onions and the pepper with olive oil, place in a roasting tin and roast in the oven for 20-30 minutes until soft and lightly coloured. When cooled, slice the onions and cut the pepper quarters into strips.

4 Beat the egg yolks, cream, milk and nutmeg in a bowl and season with salt and pepper. Line the par-cooked flan case

Overleaf Left- CREAMY ONION AND THYME FLAN, PASTA PANZANELLA *Right-* SPRING SALAD, STRAWBERRY AND BANANA CHOCOLATE TRUFFLE PAVLOVA.

with the onions. Top with the egg mixture, the cheese and decorate with the pepper strips and a few sprigs of thyme.

5 Reduce the oven temperature to 180°C (350°F), Gas Mark 4, and bake for 40 minutes, or until set and golden.

6 Serve the flan as a starter with a salad garnish. Make individual flans for slightly more special occasions.

Variations:
Replace the Spanish onions with shallots, mushrooms, peppers or tomatoes or all four. Replace the Gruyère with blue cheese or goats' cheese.

Pasta Panzanella

500 g (1 lb) your favourite dried pasta

4 tablespoons dry white or brown breadcrumbs, dry-fried until golden

2 tablespoons freshly grated Parmesan cheese (optional)

2 tablespoons pine nuts, lightly toasted

75 ml (3 fl oz) extra virgin olive oil

2 red onions, chopped

4 garlic cloves, crushed

1 bunch of basil, torn into pieces

2 tablespoons sun-dried tomato purée, or ordinary tomato purée plus a few chopped sun-dried tomatoes

250 ml (8 fl oz) white wine

fine sea salt and freshly ground black pepper

When pregnant, standing over a hot stove is most uncomfortable. This rustic Italian pasta dish is quick to make, yet satisfying. Allow 75-125 g (3-4 oz) dried pasta per person.

1 Bring a large saucepan of lightly salted water to the boil and cook the pasta for 12 minutes or according to the packet instructions, until firm to the bite.

2 Meanwhile, mix together the breadcrumbs, Parmesan and toasted pine nuts.

3 Heat the oil in a small saucepan and gently cook the chopped onions and garlic until beginning to soften. Add the basil and cook briefly before stirring in the tomato purée. When bubbling gently, add the white wine, stir well and then bring back to a simmer. Season well.

4 Pour the sauce over the pasta and serve with a good sprinkling of the breadcrumb mixture.

Variation:
Add more vegetables to the sauce such as mushrooms, peppers, tomatoes or roasted aubergines.

Spring Salad

50 g (2 oz) ripe black olives, pitted

4 pieces of sun-dried peppers in olive oil

1 carrot, cut into matchsticks, or
    4 whole baby carrots

½ fennel bulb, thinly sliced

½ red or Spanish onion, thinly sliced

mixture of oakleaf, rocket and romaine lettuce

50 g (2 oz) goats' cheese, for sprinkling (optional)

DRESSING:

1 tablespoon red wine vinegar

1 teaspoon Dijon mustard

4 tablespoons sun-dried pepper oil or extra virgin olive oil

fine sea salt and freshly ground black pepper

This salad is a nice clean and light accompaniment to pasta, quick to prepare and tasty to eat.

1 Combine all the ingredients except the cheese and arrange in a large salad bowl or on individual plates.

2 Shake the dressing ingredients together in a screw-top jar to form an emulsion. Dress the salad when ready to serve and sprinkle with the cheese, if using. Serve with chunks of fresh bread, such as ciabatta.

Strawberry and Banana Chocolate Truffle Pavlova

4 free-range egg whites (size 1)

pinch of salt

250 g (8 oz) golden caster sugar

1 teaspoon cornflour

1 teaspoon vanilla extract

1 teaspoon lemon juice

125 g (4 oz) plain Belgian chocolate or good quality real
   chocolate, broken into pieces

300 ml (½ pint) double or whipping cream

15 g (½ oz) cocoa powder

175 g (6 oz) fresh ripe strawberries

2 bananas, sliced and tossed in lemon juice to
   prevent discoloration

This recipe certainly satisfies any cravings for chocolate and feeds hungry friends at the same time. If you're following the suggested menu this dish will use up the egg whites left over from the flan.

Make the chocolate cream and decorate the pavlova literally within 1 hour of eating to avoid the meringue becoming soggy.

1 Line a baking sheet with silicone paper.

2 Whisk the egg whites in a grease-free bowl with the salt until firm. Beat in the sugar, a tablespoon at a time and continue beating until the mixture is very stiff. Fold in the cornflour, vanilla extract and lemon juice.

3 Pour the mixture on to the silicone paper and, using a spatula, spread the meringue mixture into a rough circle about 3.5 cm (1½ inches) thick. Bake for about 1 hour in a preheated oven,

140°C (275°F), Gas Mark 1, then turn off the oven and leave the meringue to finish cooking and cool down in the closed oven. Allow at least 3 hours before eating at this stage.

4 Melt the chocolate in a heatproof bowl set over a saucepan of gently simmering water and then allow to cool slightly.

5 Whip the cream in a clean bowl until soft peaks form, then add half of the melted chocolate, whipping all the time. Beat in the remaining chocolate gently until the mixture is an even colour. Spread the chocolate cream over the meringue and dust with the cocoa powder. Refrigerate for no more than 30 minutes – if you have a larder keep it in there.

6 Decorate the pavlova with the strawberries and bananas or other fruits in season and serve.

Date and Nut Loaf

a little oil, for oiling

300 ml (½ pint) boiling water

250 g (8 oz) stoned dates

1 teaspoon bicarbonate of soda

250 g (8 oz) golden caster sugar

75 g (3 oz) unsalted butter or vegan margarine

300 g (10 oz) organic wholewheat flour

1 teaspoon baking powder

½ teaspoon salt

50 g (2 oz) chopped mixed nuts (choose your favourite)

1 Grease a 1 kg (2 lb) loaf tin and line with greased greaseproof paper. Mix the boiling water, the dates and the bicarbonate of soda together in a bowl and leave to stand for 5 minutes.

2 Beat the sugar and butter until fluffy and stir in the date mixture. Sift the flour, baking powder and salt (retaining the bran) into the mixture and fold in the mixed nuts.

3 Turn the mixture into the loaf tin, smooth the top and bake in a preheated oven, 180°C (350°F), Gas Mark 4 for 1 hour.

4 Turn out and cool on a wire rack. Serve with butter.

Mid-Term Pregnancy

At this stage you will find that you will not want to stand on your feet for too long. Here are a couple of good, healthy and satisfying meals for you and your family or friends which are simple and quick to prepare.

Serves 4

Linguini and Spinach with Herby Walnut and Sun-Dried Tomato Pesto

Jolly Roger's Tipsy Cake

Linguini and Spinach with Herby Walnut and Sun-Dried Tomato Pesto

500 g (1 lb) dried linguini, tagliatelle or spaghetti

25 g (1 oz) butter

2 tablespoons olive oil

2 large onions, finely sliced

4 garlic cloves, crushed

½ teaspoon chilli powder

125 g (4 oz) chestnut mushrooms

500 g (1 lb) fresh spinach

1 tablespoon tomato purée

fine sea salt and freshly ground black pepper

PESTO:

2 tablespoons finely chopped fresh parsley

2 tablespoons torn basil leaves

2 tablespoons chopped fresh mint

3 garlic cloves, crushed

grated rind and juice of 1 lemon

3 tablespoons finely chopped walnuts

3 tablespoons Parmesan cheese, freshly grated

150 ml (¼ pint) extra virgin olive oil or sun-dried tomato oil

6 pieces of sun-dried tomatoes

The pasta you can prepare in advance; the pesto must be prepared in advance but the spinach must be cooked just before serving. However, the spinach can be prepared beforehand – washed and any large stalks or brown leaves discarded. Choose healthy, alive-looking spinach, free from any blemishes.

1 Make the pesto by combining all the ingredients in a food processor or blender. Use the 'pulse' action rather than 'blend' to ensure that the ingredients are combined gradually to form a paste, not a purée. When prepared, set aside in a cool place – not the refrigerator unless you are storing it overnight – to allow the flavours a chance to develop.

2 Bring a large saucepan of lightly salted water to the boil. Cook the pasta according to the packet instructions.

3 Meanwhile, melt the butter with the olive oil in a deep, heavy saucepan. Add the onions, garlic and chilli powder. Cover and cook gently for 5 minutes. Stir in the mushrooms and cook for another 5 minutes.

4 When the mushrooms and onions have softened stir in the spinach, cook for a further 2 minutes and then add the tomato purée. Season to taste. Continue to cook for another 2 minutes. Remove from the heat and keep covered while the pasta finishes cooking.

5 Drain the pasta and toss immediately in the pesto. Serve topped with the spinach and more Parmesan, if liked.

Jolly Roger's Tipsy Cake

300 g (10 oz) Jamaica ginger cake, broken into pieces

25 g (1 oz) preserved ginger

4 large oranges, peeled, segmented and juice retained

grated rind and juice of 1 large lemon

3 tablespoons Madeira

2 tablespoons clear honey

300 ml (½ pint) double cream

2 egg whites

fruit, to decorate, such as strawberries,
  raspberries, kiwifruit

This is one of those puddings you simply can't fail with. Easy to make, more-ish to eat. If you don't like shop bought cake, make it yourself. The ingredients seem to give it the feel of piracy on the Spanish Maine.

1 Place the cake pieces in an attractive serving bowl. Top with the ginger and oranges. (If like me, you enjoy Madeira, splosh some on top here also and perhaps trickle on some ginger syrup.)

2 Mix together the lemon rind and juice, Madeira and honey in a small bowl.

3 In another bowl, whip the cream until soft peaks form, then beat in the liquid, a little at a time, making sure that the cream retains its shape.

4 Whisk the egg whites in a clean grease-free bowl until soft peaks form then fold into the cream. Pour on top of the ginger cake and chill for at least 2 hours, before serving, decorated with your chosen fruits.

Serves 4

Warm New Potato Salad
Red Pepper and Aubergine Pie with Mushroom Ragoût
Garden Salad with Orange Vinaigrette
Gooey Chewy Chocolate Brownies and Cream

Warm New Potato Salad

500 g (1 lb) new potatoes (preferably Jersey Royals)

2 bunches of spring onions, chopped

75 g (3 oz) Stilton, dolcelatte or goats' cheese,
  crumbled (optional)

DRESSING:

2 tablespoons white wine vinegar

1 tablespoon wholegrain mustard

3 tablespoons extra virgin olive oil

2 garlic cloves, crushed (optional)

1 teaspoon demerara sugar

fine sea salt and freshly ground black pepper

A nice way to serve tiny, sweet and succulent new potatoes although it's equally good with old potatoes – just double the dressing to allow for absorption.

1 Cook the potatoes in a saucepan of salted boiling water for 15 minutes or until tender.

2 Meanwhile, make the dressing by shaking all the ingredients together in a screw-top jar.

3 When the potatoes are cooked, drain, mix with the spring onions and toss immediately in the dressing. Sprinkle the cheese over the top, if using, and serve. The salad is best eaten straight-away but is also tasty when eaten cold.

Overleaf Left- GARDEN SALAD WITH ORANGE VINAIGRETTE
Right- RED PEPPER AND AUBERGINE PIE, WARM POTATO SALAD

Red Pepper and Aubergine Pie

3 large red peppers, cored, deseeded and halved

2 large aubergines, trimmed and quartered

2 teaspoons dried oregano

2 tablespoons extra virgin olive oil, plus
   extra for brushing

1 large onion, finely chopped

50 g (2 oz) pine nuts

4 large ripe tomatoes, skinned, deseeded and
   chopped, the juice retained

1 tablespoon tomato purée

2 tablespoons chopped fresh basil

pinch of freshly grated nutmeg

500 g (1 lb) frozen puff pastry, thawed

125 g (4 oz) dolcelatte cheese, crumbled

1 egg, beaten

2 tablespoons sesame seeds

fine sea salt and freshly ground black pepper

sprigs of mint and parsley, to garnish

RAGOÛT:

75 g (3 oz) butter or 2 tablespoons olive oil

2 shallots, finely chopped

3 garlic cloves, crushed

1 teaspoon paprika

175 g (6 oz) shiitake mushrooms, roughly chopped

175 g (6 oz) chestnut mushrooms, roughly chopped

175 g (6 oz) oyster mushrooms, roughly chopped

150 ml (¼ pint) dry white wine

300 ml (½ pint) whipping cream (optional)

2 tablespoons chopped fresh parsley

This dish is extremely satisfying, best made in summer when the ingredients are at their best, although they are usually available all year round.

1 Brush the peppers and aubergines with olive oil, place them on a baking sheet. Season them and sprinkle with oregano. Roast them in a preheated oven, 220°C (425°F), Gas Mark 7, for 10 minutes, then add the pine nuts and continue roasting for another 5 minutes. Remove from the oven and allow to cool, then roughly chop the peppers and aubergines – they should not be quite cooked at this stage.

2 Heat the olive oil in a large pan, add the onion and cook for 5 minutes. Add the aubergines, peppers and pine nuts. Cook for 1 minute before stirring in the tomatoes. Bring the mixture quickly to the boil, stirring frequently to avoid burning. Add the tomato purée and cook for 1 minute. Finally, add the basil, nutmeg and seasoning and set aside to cool.

3 Roll out the puff pastry on a lightly floured cold surface to form a 30 cm (12 inch) square. Spoon the vegetable filling into the centre leaving a border 5 cm (2 inches) wide. Top with the crumbled cheese. With a knife cut diagonal strips, 3.5 cm (1½ inches) long, down each side of the mixture. Tuck the ends over to form a plait.

4 Transfer the pie to a greased baking sheet, brush with beaten egg and sprinkle with sesame seeds. Allow to rest for 30 minutes in the refrigerator before baking.

5 Bake in a preheated oven, 220°C (425°F), Gas Mark 7, for 15 minutes then reduce the temperature to 190°C (375°F), Gas Mark 5, for at least another 15 minutes or until golden brown and risen.

6 To make the sauce, melt 40 g (1½ oz) of the butter or 1 tablespoon of the oil in a pan. Add the shallots, garlic and paprika and cook until beginning to soften. Stir in the shiitake and chestnut mushrooms and cook for 2 minutes.

7 Add the remaining butter or olive oil and when hot stir in the oyster mushrooms. Cook for 2 minutes and when the mixture is very hot add the wine and reduce by two thirds.

8 Pour in the cream, if using, and gently bring to the boil. Allow it to bubble away until reduced by half and thickened to a coating consistency. The sauce is now ready so stir in the parsley and serve with the pie.

Garden Salad with Orange Vinaigrette

250 g (8 oz) fresh peas

4 bunches of watercress, stalks removed

1 orange, peeled and segmented

20 fresh mint leaves, finely chopped

DRESSING:

2 tablespoons freshly squeezed orange juice

1 tablespoon lemon juice

grated rind of 2 oranges

pinch of sugar (optional)

3 tablespoons walnut oil

3 tablespoons safflower oil

fine sea salt and freshly ground black pepper

This is a really racy, fresh and vibrant salad to rejuvenate your tastebuds and is an excellent accompaniment to new potatoes in any meal. If fresh peas are unavailable, use frozen petit pois, mangetout, sugar snaps, or fresh green beans or even barely cooked asparagus tips.

1 Cook the peas in a saucepan of salted boiling water for a few minutes. Drain well and mix with the watercress and orange segments; seasoning to taste. Arrange in a salad bowl.

2 Make the dressing by shaking all the ingredients together in a screw-top jar. Dress the salad liberally just before serving.

Gooey Chewy Chocolate Brownies

a little oil, for oiling

625 g (1¼ lb) plain chocolate, broken into pieces

250 g (8 oz) unsalted butter, diced

2 tablespoons fresh, strong coffee

175 g (6 oz) demerara or caster sugar

3 free-range eggs, beaten

75 g (3 oz) unbleached plain white flour

1 teaspoon baking powder

½ teaspoon fine sea salt

175 g (6 oz) raisins, or half raisins and half walnuts

1 teaspoon vanilla extract

This excellent recipe will serve you throughout your life; you'll use it time and time again for all your family and friends.

The brownies are good hot or cold for a main meal or as a snack. Remember any brownie is only as good as the chocolate you use. Good chocolate contains nothing less than 35% cocoa solids – if you can, buy 70% cocoa solids – the flavour is truly remarkable.

1 Grease and line a 20 x 28 cm (8 x 11 inch) baking tray.

2 Melt the chocolate and butter in a heatproof bowl over a saucepan of gently boiling water.

3 While the coffee is hot add the sugar to it, making sure it dissolves. When cool beat in the eggs.

4 Combine the remaining ingredients together in a bowl. Add the melted chocolate to the egg mixture and combine together well. Fold into the dry ingredients.

5 Pour the mixture into the prepared tin and bake in a preheated oven, 190°C (375°F), Gas Mark 5 for about 45 minutes or until just firm to the touch.

6 Cut into squares and serve warm with cream and/or hot chocolate sauce.

TEN-MINUTE MEALS FOR HEAVILY PREGNANT WOMEN

When you are huge – and this can happen at any time from 7 months onwards – the last thing you will want to do is spend hours over a hot stove. The key words here are 'speed', 'simplicity' and 'single pan' – you don't want to spend hours washing up either! If you are cooking just for yourself then the quantities will be small, too, as you'll probably want six small meals throughout the day, rather than three larger ones.

The recipes given are all for 4 people but you may well find yourself cooking one tasty dish and saving the remainder for future meals. It is highly unlikely that you will attempt to cook puddings but will prefer instead cut-up fruits, yogurts and fromage frais, plus, of course, the occasional square or, more likely, bar of pure chocolate.

In the month or two before giving birth meals must remain highly nutritious and quality, not quantity, is most important. Here are five small, tasty and healthy meals suitable for a day in late-term pregnancy.

Chinese Noodles, Peppers and Tofu

275 g (9 oz) Chinese egg noodles

1 tablespoon sesame oil

4 spring onions, chopped

2 garlic cloves, crushed

1 teaspoon Szechuan chilli powder

1 large red pepper, cored, deseeded and
  cut into strips

1 large yellow pepper, cored, deseeded and
  cut into strips

125 g (4 oz) firm tofu, cut into 1 cm (½ inch) cubes

175 g (6 oz) sugar snaps or mangetout,
  topped and tailed

175 g (6 oz) sprouted seeds

2 tablespoons chopped fresh sweet basil

25 g (1 oz) fresh root ginger, grated

1 tablespoon shoyu

fine sea salt and freshly ground black pepper

Not only is this a fast highly nutritious feast, it looks good too. So what's the difference between noodles and pasta? Noodles usually have eggs in them while pasta doesn't necessarily. I am particularly fond of bean thread or cellophane noodles. These are made from bean gelatine and are vegan, and make a good filler for spring rolls. You can adapt the recipe to whatever you have in your store cupboard. Dry noodles or pasta will keep almost indefinitely in a cool dry place. Some oriental noodles need soaking prior to use – 30 minutes in cold water is more than adequate.

Sweet basil is a relative of ordinary basil but it is one fresh herb which complements oriental cooking perfectly. It is often available from Chinese supermarkets – if you can't get sweet basil use ordinary basil or coriander instead.

1 Cook the noodles according to the packet instructions.

2 Meanwhile, heat the oil in a wok or large frying pan. When the oil is very hot, add the onions, garlic and chilli powder. Stir-fry for 30 seconds before adding the peppers and tofu. Cook for 4 minutes.

3 When the noodles are ready to be drained and served toss the sugar snaps or mangetout, sprouted seeds, sweet basil

and ginger into the wok and stir-fry for 1 further minute before adding the shoyu and seasoning. Stir in the noodles, mix well and serve immediately.

Serves 4

Fragrant Carrot and Cannellini Soup

2 tablespoons extra virgin olive oil

1 large onion, chopped

2 garlic cloves, crushed

2 teaspoons cumin seeds

500 g (1 lb) carrots, topped
   and tailed and sliced

1 large potato, chopped

1.2 litres (2 pints) hot vegetable stock

125 g (4 oz) dried cannellini beans, soaked
   overnight and cooked according to the
   packet instructions (see note below)

fine sea salt and freshly ground black pepper

a little natural yogurt, soured cream, crème fraîche
   or grated cheese, to serve (optional)

1 bunch of fresh coriander, chopped, to garnish

There's nothing better than a good soup in times of distress. When you are pregnant a good quick soup is an ideal meal. Soups can always be extended or added to, to make a more substantial meal.

1 Heat the olive oil in a large heavy saucepan. Add the onion and sauté gently for 2 minutes. Stir in the garlic and cumin seeds and allow the seeds to cook well. Add the carrots and potato and cook for a further 3 minutes. Pour in the vegetable stock and bring back to the boil, then reduce the heat to a simmer.

2 When all the vegetables are tender, purée them in a liquidizer or food processor, or rub them through a sieve.

Adjust the consistency of the soup by adding a little more stock or water if necessary, and season well with salt and freshly ground black pepper.

3 Return the soup to the rinsed saucepan, add the cooked cannellini beans and heat gently, stirring occasionally.

4 To serve, add a dollop of yogurt, soured cream, crème fraîche or a little grated cheese, if liked, and sprinkle with chopped fresh coriander. Serve immediately with your favourite croûtons and organic wholewheat bread.

Serves 4

Note:
When cooking any dried beans that need soaking, boil them vigorously for 10 minutes prior to soaking overnight and skim off any impurities that rise to the surface. When finally cooked, these beans will be very easy to digest.

Spicy Lentils

1 tablespoon sunflower oil

2 garlic cloves, crushed

1 red onion, chopped

1 large carrot, grated

1 teaspoon garam masala

1 teaspoon fennel seeds

1 teaspoon cumin seeds

1 teaspoon coriander seeds, crushed

625 g (1¼ lb) red lentils

425 g (14 oz) can chopped tomatoes

fine sea salt and freshly ground black pepper

1 bunch of fresh coriander or basil, chopped,
   to garnish

When Kate was pregnant with Mollie I would quite often find her cooking something like this. On asking her why she would reply that she just fancied lentils – good old basic lentils. They are very quick to cook, full of protein and they are surprisingly more-ish. This dish would make a good accompaniment to a more elaborate curry but stands on it's own, too. If you're not in the mood for spice then simply omit it and rename the dish!

1 Heat the oil in a large heavy saucepan. Add the garlic, onion, carrot and spices and stir-fry for about 5 minutes. Add the red lentils and stir-fry for a further 3 minutes. Stir in the chopped tomatoes and enough water to cover the lentils and leave it to simmer on top of the stove for about 30 minutes. Alternatively, transfer the lentils to a baking dish and finish cooking them in the oven on a low heat.

2 Season to taste and serve the lentils topped with chopped coriander or basil.

Serves 4

Variations:

If cooking in the oven top the lentils with a little grated cheese. If liked, sweeten the dish naturally by adding a few sultanas or raisins.

A variation for a simple yet delicious alternative to Spicy Lentils. (See page 52.) Heat 1 tablespoon sunflower oil in a large heavy saucepan. Add the crushed garlic and the chopped red onion and stir-fry until the onion starts to blacken. Add the red lentils and cook for another 3 minutes, then add the canned chopped tomatoes and cook as before. This method of cooking red lentils produces a wonderful smoky flavour but may not appeal to everyone; especially children.

Tim's Spanish Tortilla

1 tablespoon extra virgin olive oil
1 red onion, finely sliced
1 garlic clove, crushed
1 red pepper, cored, deseeded and diced
1 green pepper, cored, deseeded and diced
250 g (8 oz) cooked waxy potatoes
4 free-range eggs (size 1), beaten
fine sea salt and freshly ground black pepper

I don't know why but I always feel a bit strange writing recipes that are so well known. But Spanish Tortillas are invariably cooked badly. We started cooking Spanish Tortillas at the restaurant when Tim (our Head Chef's boyfriend) suggested that it might be a good breakfast food. He is somewhat of a 'Spanophile' and he makes a jolly good tortilla. Quick to make, tortillas are nutritious and attractive and just as good hot or cold. They're also excellent for using up leftovers especially vegetable leftovers. What you need is a well-loved cast-iron frying pan or tortilla pan, free from any residual baked-on food. If you are going to be cooking for just yourself and, of course, your 'lump' then it is well worth investing in an individual tortilla pan.

Spaniards like their tortillas undercooked – although this is not recommended for pregnant women – and will often eat them like a sandwich between hunks of fresh crusty bread.

1 Heat the oil in your frying or tortilla pan. Add the onion, garlic and peppers and cook for 3 minutes. Remove from the heat and tip the vegetables into a bowl. Add the eggs, mix in well, season then return the mixture to the frying pan.

2 Cook over a moderate heat until set then gently ease the omelette away from the sides of the pan with a spatula and with the help of a suitably sized plate turn the omelette over so the other side can colour. Cook for 1 further minute then serve.

Serves 4

Steamed Baby Vegetables with Lime and Walnut Dressing

250 g (8 oz) baby Jersey Royal potatoes, whole

250 g (8 oz) baby carrots with green tops still attached

250 g (8 oz) baby courgettes, courgette flowers still attached

125 g (4 oz) tender asparagus tips

250 g (8 oz) baby corn

125 g (4 oz) sugar snaps

DRESSING:

1 shallot, finely chopped

1 tablespoon clear honey

2 tablespoons freshly squeezed lime juice

6 tablespoons walnut oil

½ teaspoon mustard powder

fine sea salt and freshly ground black pepper

You will only be able to make this dish at certain times of the year, depending on the seasonal availability of some of the vegetables.

If you can't afford a proper steaming outfit measure your large saucepans and find a cheap Chinese bamboo one that will fit – they cost very little.

This is a lovely dish to make just for yourself although you must be careful to undercook any vegetables that you are going to re-heat later in the day.

1 Bring a large saucepan of salted water to the boil. Add the whole potatoes and cook for 14 minutes or until tender.

2 Meanwhile, set up your Chinese bamboo steamer above the potatoes. They usually have at least 2 levels. After about 8 minutes put the whole baby carrots in the bottom level nearest the steam. After 3 minutes add the whole courgettes to the carrots and place the asparagus tips, whole baby corn and sugar snaps in the top layer. With any luck they should all be ready when the potatoes are cooked.

3 While the vegetables are steaming, make the dressing simply by mixing the dressing ingredients together very well.

4 Serve the vegetables with a good spoonful of vinaigrette on hot plates (simply cooked vegetables such as these will go cold very quickly otherwise).

Serves 4

Variation:
Try other vegetables like baby cauliflower, runner beans, broad beans, baby turnips and parsnips, baby leeks, baby aubergines and even cherry tomatoes.

A BABY!

At last he or she has arrived and all that matters is that the baby is healthy, happy and, ideally breastfed. I won't push the point, whole books have been written on the subject; but, to put it in a nutshell, infant preparations could be classed as cheap 'plonk' while breast milk is vintage champagne. Having said that, many mothers cannot breastfeed for a variety of reasons and so must take even more care when the time for introducing solids comes.

For the first 3-5 days of a baby's life he or she will be sucking colostrum from their mother's breast. It is very high in Vitamin A and new-born babies need it to develop healthy mucous linings in the eyes, nose and lungs. A baby who receives this colostrum is less likely to develop bronchial infections, so even if long-term breastfeeding is not an option it's worth battling away for the first week to make sure the baby has its fair share of Vitamin A. It is widely recognised that most of our natural immune systems develop better in breastfed babies than in bottle-fed babies. A breastfed baby will also be better equipped to move on to solids gradually when the time comes, simply because they will find they can eat a wider variety of things with little or no allergic reaction. One good reason for this is because breast milk will gradually be gently flavoured by what the mother is eating and drinking. It may well be that mothers with gastronomical tastes develop gastronomically aware babies through their breast milk. Infant preparations just can't compete!

Times vary but from 4-6 months there will come a stage when your baby is definitely looking for a little extra snack. If your supply of milk is copious you are unlikely to notice this so much but you may be noticing that feeding sessions are getting longer and longer. If your milk supply is not so prolific and you are already adding a feed of infant preparation then it looks like the time has come to let some new tastebuds loose on the world of food.

Initially you will give your baby a little extra at the end of a normal feed. As the demand for more increases there will come a point, and only you can judge it, when the extra comes first and the breast comes second. You've achieved the first step in weaning your baby. There are some very important things to remember when introducing your baby to solids.

1 Do not give your baby refined sugar in any shape or form – it is not worth even using honey (75% sugar) at this stage. The human body has no need of it; it is addictive and is better for your baby's tastebuds not to recognize it.

2 Do not give your newborn any extra salt. Too much salt in a baby's diet will damage the kidneys. Many pre-prepared baby foods contain more salt than is necessary.

3 Remember your baby's body is still growing and developing, he or she may not be able to cope with some foods yet especially if bottle-fed. Allergic reactions to basic foods can continue throughout childhood but particularly up to the age of five. To help identify any rogue foods it's worth, while still partially breast-feeding, giving your baby purées of single foods, perhaps with your own milk, cow's milk or soya milk.

Six Months Plus

As I said at the beginning of the chapter, cooking is an act of love and caring – what is more important at this stage of your child's life than food prepared by his own mother or father. Prepared foods are great in emergencies or when travelling but as a rule, cook for your baby yourself whenever possible. By cooking you will remain in touch with what is probably the most important time in a child's development. Babies have excellent natural palates and will appreciate a wide range of natural flavours after several months of eating nothing but milk, albeit flavoured by mum. New tastes will be great adventures and one thing is for sure, if the customer in this case does not like his meal he will quickly and efficiently reject it! Babies thrive on fresh, lightly cooked vegetables, ripe raw fruits (not strawberries or citrus fruits early on) and easily digested protein such as egg yolk, tofu, curd cheese, yogurt, fromage frais, wholewheat cereals and beans and pulses.

Avoid added fats as far as you can but do use full-fat milk and butter where needed rather than semi-skimmed milk or chemically produced margarines. In fact, where necessary use unrefined cold pressed oils if you can. At six months though these items don't really come into the equation. The following are some of the basic foodstuffs with tips on how to use them.

1. Milks

a) Cows' milk should be introduced really carefully. If introduced too soon it will upset a baby's allergic system. It should never be given to babies under six months. Seven to eight months is an ideal time to use it, for softening purées of various foods and as a supplement to breast milk. Cows' milk should always be boiled before being given to a baby.

b) Soya milk is a good substitute for cows' milk and is suitable for use with a six-month-old baby. It may lack a few of the vitamins here and there but you can always make those up with fresh vegetables and fruit.

c) Goats' or ewes' milk is probably not worth using with vegetarian babies as both milks lack a lot of important vitamins. The best thing about these milks is their low sodium content.

2. Milk products

Yogurt and fromage frais are both excellent sources of protein and calcium. The bacteria they contain also aids young babies' digestive systems, helping to avoid stomach upsets. Yogurt and fromage frais may be used on their own from six months onwards or can be diluted with sterile water. They can also be added to fruit or vegetable purées as can soft cheeses such as quark, ricotta and mascarpone. Avoid soft cheeses with rinds and goats' or ewes' cheeses.

Cheese is another milk product that your baby will enjoy. Use mild vegetarian Cheddar or curd cheese – try to avoid vacuum-packed soft cheeses. Cheese should never be overcooked as your baby will not be able to digest it. Use it combined with vegetables, grains, beans or fruit.

3. Eggs, grains, beans and bean products

These are essential building blocks for your baby. If you don't eat eggs I would recommend substituting tofu instead. It is almost as good nutritionally although not quite so versatile and yet much easier to digest.

Eggs, of course, must be well cooked and babies under eight months should not be given egg whites. Always buy fresh free-range eggs with a recent packaging date.

Cereals and grains should be added to the baby's diet with as much caution as milk and milk products. Rice is probably the best to start with. Use organic brown rice ideally as it has a very low incidence of allergic reaction, compared to wheat and wheat products. If you are able, use ground rice initially as it takes much less time to cook and is easier for the baby to digest. Cereals supply vital energy for your baby with important vitamins, nutrients, trace elements, plus the all important protection of dietary fibre. Don't go mad though, very young digestive systems can only cope with a meal that is high in cereal fibre, once a day. Also use porridge oats – a wonderful traditional cereal, nourishing, palatable and superb for a quick, healthy breakfast. Properly prepared beans and pulses are an excellent source of protein and other nutrients for babies of six months and older. All are easy to purée and combine well with other foods.

4. Fresh fruit and vegetables

These are all vital for life, with their vitamins, minerals and, of course, fibre. Avoid canned fruits and vegetables with the exception of some beans and pulses, sweetcorn, tomatoes and unsweetened fruit – if desperate. Baked beans are best made at home where you can control the sugar content. Most fresh fruit needs little or no cooking. Vegetables of course vary but if given the option always tend to undercook or leave raw succulent or leafy vegetables. Some root vegetables and tubers must be properly cooked but not cooked to death. If you can, buy high-quality organic foods. Always buy good, firm, undamaged produce. Encourage your baby to eat fruit and vegetable skins as long as they have been well washed and cooked if necessary. Frozen fruits are excellent substitutes when fresh fruit is not in season and variety is essential to stimulate your baby's appetite. Dried fruits make marvellous healthy snacks as your baby gets older but because they are lower in vitamins and higher in sugar content than fresh fruit they are best used as a sweetener for young babies' desserts, should it be necessary. Fruit spreads with no added sugar are excellent for flavouring yogurts, soft cheeses and cereal puddings.

5. Seeds and nuts

Babies must not eat whole seeds or nuts but they can be ground or turned into spreads and then added to dishes. Peanut and other nut butters, tahini (sesame seed paste) or sunflower paste, are all ideal products.

6. Drinks

Apart from breast milk, try water (sterilized until the baby is six months old), diluted freshly squeezed and strained juices from fruits and vegetables and any unsweetened fruit juice (all our children developed an early addiction to unsweetened, diluted apple juice). Fruit juice can be diluted to 1 part juice to 8 parts water, gradually increasing the strength as your child gets older. All fruit juices should be used within 2-3 days once opened.

7. Pasta

Pasta is an ideal food product for small babies. To begin with mash cooked, wholewheat, organic pasta with the rest of your ingredients. As the baby gets older, simply chop it up and the baby or toddler will be able to eat whole pasta – the smaller varieties like gnocchetti or tubetti are the most suitable.

A TYPICAL DAILY MENU
FOR A 6 TO 18-MONTH-OLD BABY

At this age the weaning process will probably have gently started. Most babies will be sleeping through the night so meal times will bear much more relation to adult meal times. The child's tastebuds will have been awakened by the occasional purée offered before breastfeeding in the preceding two months. Start to introduce tiny amounts of onion, garlic and herbs into the meals.

It is most important to watch your baby at all times when he is feeding at this age as it is very easy for babies to choke on small pieces of food. Equally though as the teeth develop so your baby should be given every opportunity to use them. This phase of your child's life really covers the transition from baby food to family food. By 18 months most children will be eating cut up versions of the elder brother's and sister's food. If he or she is your first child then get into the habit of setting aside portions of your own food before you add loads of chilli or Parmesan cheese!

Avocado, tofu, tahini, fromage frais, yogurt, red lentils and pasta all make an ideal basis for quick meals if you are in a hurry and can often be extended into something for yourself.

It is also important to pay as much attention as possible to the colour and texture of your baby's food, for as their senses develop so do their demands on you to provide not just tasty food but nice looking food as well. All too often baby food is presented as a bland mass of gluey looking mush.

TYPICAL MENU FOR A 6-18-MONTH-OLD BABY

ON WAKING FIRST THING: Very diluted apple juice, warm or cold (not chilled)

BREAKFAST 8-9 AM
Winter: Porridge Oats with Fresh Apple and Fromage Frais
Summer: Baby Muesli with Fresh Peach Purée and Yogurt

to drink: Breast or diluted cows' milk, or diluted juice

LUNCH 12-1.30 PM
Winter: Cauliflower and Pasta Cheese
                         Fruit and Vegetable Crudités
                         Plum and Tahini Custard Cream
Summer: Lentil and Vegetable Ragoût
                         Breadsticks (Grissini)
                         Raspberry and Tofu Cream

to drink: Diluted fruit or milk drink

TEA 3.30-5.30 PM
Winter: Butter Bean Winter Warmer
                         Cut-Up Avocado
                         Pear and Nut Crumble
Summer: Fresh Spinach Risotto
                         Baby Hummus
                         Fresh Nectarine Fromage Frais
to drink: Breast or diluted cows' milk

BEDTIME 6-7 PM   Breast or diluted cows' milk

Porridge Oats with Fresh Apple and Fromage Frais

4 tablespoons cows' or soya milk

1 heaped tablespoon rolled oats

1 Cox's Orange Pippin or other small dessert apple, peeled, cored and grated

1 tablespoon plain fromage frais

This is a very simple breakfast, but very nutritious and perfect for cold winter mornings. If you're worried about the size of the rolled oats, give them a good 'whizz' in a liquidizer or food processor.

1 Bring the milk to the boil in a stainless steel saucepan. Sprinkle on the oats, bring back to the boil, then simmer for 1 minute.

2 Stir in the grated apple and cook for a further 3 minutes. If it is a little dry, add 2 tablespoons of water. Serve topped with a small dollop of fromage frais.

Serves 1 very small person

Variations:

Replace the apple with other fruit such as pears or plums, or a fruit purée, a nut or seed butter or a little of both.

Fresh fruit purées for babies are made by mixing fruit with water or milk or both. Hard fruits should be lightly cooked or grated; soft fruits can be pulped. In all cases stones, seeds and indigestible or blemished skins should be removed. If the fruit used is too acidic, sweeten it with a little date purée or natural fruit juice concentrate. Date purée is made by cooking natural dates in a little water then sieving or liquidizing them.

Dried fruit purées are excellent for making 'instant' purées. In most cases soak the fruit overnight then poach for 30 minutes or until tender. Save the water from the cooking to soften the purée or to offer as a drink. When the fruit is cooked, drain before liquidizing or sieving. Good dried fruits for puréeing are apples, apricots, dates, figs, prunes, raisins and sultanas.

Baby Muesli with Fresh Peach Purée and Yogurt

1 teaspoon wheatgerm

1 tablespoon rolled oats

1 tablespoon sunflower seeds

1 teaspoon seedless raisins

1 tablespoon cashew nuts

5 tablespoons milk or water

1 ripe peach, skinned, halved and stoned

1 tablespoon natural yogurt

Baby muesli is best made at home. Avoid using wheat products initially, then as your baby grows introduce them gradually. For small babies, you must 'whizz' the dry ingredients in a liquidizer or food processor prior to use.

1 Combine the dry ingredients, cover with the milk or water and soak for 10 minutes, or bring to the boil in a small saucepan and simmer for 5 minutes. Older babies can eat the muesli uncooked with either hot or cold milk.

2 Mash the peach then mix with a fork. Combine the peach and muesli and serve topped with natural yogurt. If a little dry serve with extra milk.

Serves 1 very small person

Variations:

Vary the dry ingredients, try ground rice, maize meal or millet (all should be cooked), or add nut or seed pastes like peanut butter or tahini. Substitute sultanas, dates or figs for raisins.

Try other additions such as any fruit purée, grated fresh hard fruit, fromage frais, soya milk, quark or even a homemade fruity yogurt.

Overleaf Left- CAULIFLOWER AND PASTA CHEESE, PLUM AND TAHINI CUSTARD CREAM *Right-* CRUDITÉS

Cauliflower and Pasta Cheese

75 g (3 oz) cauliflower, broken into small florets

25 g (1 oz) organic wholewheat pasta (the smallest
size available)

3 tablespoons cows' or soya milk

1 heaped teaspoon baby rice

1 tablespoon vegetarian mild Cheddar
cheese, grated

1 teaspoon wheatgerm

There is little necessity to use ready-made meals from jars or packets and you will feel much happier knowing your baby is eating good fresh food full of natural goodness such as this. (It is suitable for younger babies if liquidized.)

1 Poach the cauliflower in a little boiling water in a saucepan for 8 minutes. Save the water and cook the pasta in it according to the packet instructions.

2 Meanwhile, bring the milk to the boil in another saucepan, add the baby rice, stir and simmer until it thickens. Remove from the heat and add the cheese, cooked cauliflower and pasta.

3 Depending on your baby it may be necessary to mash the mixture a little. Otherwise, sprinkle it with wheatgerm and place under a preheated grill for 1 minute to colour slightly.

Serves 1 very small person

Variations:

Vegans could replace the cheese with tofu.

Try using other vegetables such as broccoli, leeks, courgettes, mushrooms (for older babies only), spinach and fresh peas. The pasta can be replaced with almost any grain, bean or pulse your baby likes.

Try adding small amounts of garlic, nutmeg or herbs. The dish could also be enriched by a hard-boiled egg yolk.

Crudités

COOKED CRUDITÉS:

cauliflower florets

broccoli florets

kohlrabi, cut into sticks

artichoke hearts, halved

asparagus spears, cut into
small sections lengthways

fennel, lightly poached
and dissected

celery, cut into small lengths

courgettes, as above

parsnips, as above

carrots, as above

celeriac, as above

potato, as above

RAW CRUDITÉS:

gem lettuce

Chinese leaf ribs

tomatoes, skinned, deseeded and chopped

peppers, skinned, cored, deseeded and cut
into strips

avocados, stoned and sliced

mushrooms, whole

apples, peeled, cored and sliced

apricots, stoned

banana, sliced

cherries, pitted

grapes, deseeded and halved

mango, stoned and cut into strips

melon, sliced

peach, stoned

pear, peeled, cored and sliced

Sticks of vegetables are great for your baby's first attempts at self-sufficiency. As early as six months some babies will show an inclination to feed themselves. Because they have few teeth, if any, they must be supervised since they are inclined to choke. Vegetable strips may be cooked to aid the eating process initially. As soon as you can, reduce or eliminate the cooking.

You'll soon learn which vegetables and fruits your baby prefers – keep experimenting and eliminate the unpopular ones.

Note that waxed skins on fruit and vegetables can be de-waxed only by soaking in hot water. If this is too much trouble, remove the skin.

For 1 very small person

Plum and Tahini Custard Cream

3 large ripe plums, peeled, halved and pitted
1 teaspoon date syrup or date purée (see page 61)
1 egg yolk (size 1) vegans can use 1 teaspoon soya flour
　plus 2 teaspoons maize flour
175 ml (6 fl oz) full-fat milk or soya milk, brought to
　the boil
1 teaspoon tahini
tiny pinch of freshly grated nutmeg

It is well worth making fruit purées when fruit are in season (see page 61). They are inexpensive, filling, nutritious and a real treat for the whole family when nothing interesting is available. Babies are particularly appreciative of new flavours and textures.
1 Mash the plums with a fork and add the date syrup or purée.
2 Beat the egg or flours, if using, boiling milk, tahini and nutmeg together in a small saucepan. Combine all the ingredients well and bring back to a gentle boil, simmer for 3 minutes.
3 Pour into 4 ramekins, cover with foil and stand in an ovenproof dish containing enough hot water to cover half the depth of the ramekins. Cook in a preheated oven, 160°C (325°F), Gas Mark 3, until set, about 25 minutes. Serve chilled.
Serves 4

Lentil and Vegetable Ragoût

2 tablespoons brown lentils
2 canned or fresh tomatoes, skinned, deseeded
　and chopped
1 teaspoon grated onion – only for older babies
1 tablespoon tomato juice, or juice from the
　canned tomatoes
2 tablespoons water
50 g (2 oz) carrots, finely diced
25 g (1 oz) courgettes, finely diced
1 tablespoon sweetcorn
1 basil leaf, torn into pieces
1 tablespoon vegetarian mild Cheddar cheese, grated
　(optional)
1 tablespoon organic wholewheat breadcrumbs,
　finely ground

This is a real treat for those tiny tastebuds and it looks good too.
1 Soak and precook the lentils: boil quickly in a large pan of water for 10 minutes; remove from the heat, soak for 12 hours, then cook until tender for about 40 minutes.
2 In another pan, bring the tomatoes, onion, if using, tomato juice and water to the boil. Add the carrots, cook for 10 minutes then stir in the courgettes, sweetcorn, lentils and basil and simmer for another 10 minutes – all the vegetables should now be tender.
3 For very young babies liquidize or mash the mixture. Pour into a greased baking dish and top with the cheese, if using, and the breadcrumbs. Place under a preheated grill until golden.
Serves 1 very small person

Variations:
Use other dried beans, cereals or pulses – haricot and kidney beans are especially good but make sure they are well cooked.
　Try fresh vegetables such as green beans, mushrooms (for

older babies only), cauliflower or broccoli.

Try enhancing the sauce with nut or seed butters and pastes such as peanut butter or tahini, or you could enrich the sauce with a little milk, cream cheese or yogurt.

Breadsticks (Grissini)

1 teaspoon active dried yeast

200 g (7 oz) unbleached white bread flour, plus 1 tablespoon

12 tablespoons warm water

1 teaspoon unsalted butter, at room temperature

2 teaspoons extra virgin olive oil, plus extra for oiling

fine sea salt

Bread sticks are perfect for babies to munch, once you have established they are not allergic to wheat. What is more, these breadsticks are sugar-free which is more than can be said for shop-bought ones.

1 In a small clean bowl mix the yeast with the 1 tablespoon of flour and add 3 tablespoons of the water. Cover and set aside in a warm place to start frothing.

2 In a large clean bowl mix together the remaining flour with a good pinch of salt, then form a well in the centre of the flour. Add the yeast mixture, then the remaining water gradually working it well into the flour by hand or with a wooden spoon. When all the liquid has been absorbed knead the dough quickly, turning the bowl at the same time. It will take about 4 minutes and you will know that you have achieved the right consistency when the dough stops sticking to the sides of the bowl.

3 Place the dough on a lightly floured surface and knead it again for up to 20 minutes – yes, it is a long time and quite exhausting!

4 Return the dough to the cleaned bowl and form a well in the centre. Add half of the butter and 1 teaspoon of the oil and gradually work in. Initially the dough will fall apart; keep it up – it will come good in the end.

5 Lift the dough out of the bowl. Use the remaining oil to grease the bowl and replace the dough. Turn the dough in the bowl so that it is coated in a thin layer of olive oil. Place a damp tea towel over the bowl and leave in a warm place for about 1 hour, or until doubled in bulk.

6 Turn the dough out on to a lightly floured surface and knock back a few times before spreading it out with your fingers to form a rectangle, about 10 x 15 cm (6 x 4 inches). Fold about 1 cm (½ inch) of the longest edge towards you and then tightly roll the whole thing up to form a Swiss roll. Tuck the final edge into the bottom of the roll to make a neat seam. Brush with oil, cover and set aside to rise again for 1 hour or again, until doubled in bulk.

7 Oil a baking sheet. Cut the roll crossways into twelve 5 mm (¼ inch) lengths.

8 Hold the ends of each piece of dough and gradually pull, stretching each piece into a breadstick about 30 cm (12 inches) long. Lay each stick on the baking sheet about 2.5 cm (1 inch) apart. Spray generously with water and place immediately in the hottest part of a preheated oven, 220°C (425°F), Gas Mark 7. Bake for 6 minutes then spray again and bake for a further 20 minutes or until golden brown and crisp all the way through. Remove from the oven and allow to cool on a wire rack.

9 Breadsticks will keep in an airtight jar in a dark cool place for several weeks.

Makes 12

Raspberry and Tofu Cream

1 heaped tablespoon fresh or frozen raspberries, thawed
½ teaspoon organic apple juice concentrate
50 g (2 oz) soft tofu
1 tablespoon Greek yogurt, natural yogurt or
   crème fraîche
a little full-fat milk

Tofu is an excellent, nutritious and easily digestible food for babies. Try this with a delicious fresh fruit purée (see page 61).
1 Push the raspberries through a sieve to remove any pips. Add the rest of the ingredients and mash or blend in a liquidizer or food processor to the desired consistency.
Serves 1 very small person

Variations:
Use any soft fruit, uncooked, or any hard fruit which has been gently poached. Sweeten with date purée (see page 61) or a little honey or even fructose.
*   Try adding a little curd cheese or baby rice, or add banana as a sweetener or simply as a filler.*

Cut-Up Avocado

½ a firm avocado

Avocados are a perfect meal for young babies. (All of our children have enjoyed them.) Six to eight-month-old babies can easily eat half a ripe avocado.
1 Halve the avocado leaving the stone intact in one half.
2 Remove the skin from the stoned half and cut into finger food or simply serve directly from the skin with a teaspoon.
Serves 1 very small person

Variations:
Very ripe avocados may be puréed with a little lemon or lime juice. Alternatively, combine an avocado with cheese, fromage frais, yogurt, nut or seed pastes or even fruit purées – cooked where necessary.

Butter Bean Winter Warmer

125 ml (4 fl oz) water
50 g (2 oz) carrots, finely diced
50 g (2 oz) parsnips, finely diced
2 teaspoons finely chopped onion (only for babies over
   8 months)
25 g (1 oz) celery, finely diced
2 button mushrooms
4 tablespoons well cooked butter beans
pinch of dried thyme

It can get chilly lying in a pram in mid-winter while parents are shopping so here's a dish to provide some natural central heating.
1 Bring the water to the boil in a saucepan, add the carrots and parsnips and simmer for 10 minutes. Add the rest of the ingredients and simmer until tender. Serve the dish as is, or purée or part-purée the vegetables before serving.
Serves 1 very small person (over 8 months old)

Variation:
This dish can be enriched with milk, cream cheese or yogurt.

Pear and Nut Crumble

sunflower oil, for oiling

1 small, ripe Conference pear, peeled, cored
  and sliced

a few drops of lemon juice

½ teaspoon organic apple concentrate

1 tablespoon ground almonds

1 tablespoon organic wholewheat flour

pinch of ground cinnamon

1 teaspoon unsalted butter or cold-pressed oil

This dish can be enjoyed by the whole family.

1 Lightly oil a 1.5 cm (¼ inch) ramekin with sunflower oil. Layer the pear in the bottom of the ramekin. Sprinkle with the lemon juice and apple concentrate and enough hot water to half cover the fruit.

2 Place the ground almonds, flour, cinnamon and butter in a bowl. Rub together with the fingertips until the mixture resembles fine breadcrumbs. Sprinkle over the pear and bake in a preheated oven, 180°C (350°F), Gas Mark 4, for 45 minutes.

Serves 1 small person

Variations:
Substitute the pear with apples, peaches, apricots and almost any properly poached fruit. Add dried fruit such as chopped dates or sultanas to naturally sweeten and add regular oats or oatmeal to the crumble mix.

Fresh Spinach Risotto

4 tablespoons boiling water

1 tablespoon Basmati or other long-grain white
  rice, washed and well drained

1 fresh tomato, skinned, deseeded and chopped

1 teaspoon finely chopped onion (optional)

50 g (2 oz) fresh spinach, roughly chopped and
  large stalks removed

1 tablespoon grated vegetarian mild Cheddar
  cheese, or crumbled tofu

2 teaspoons cream cheese or fromage frais

This exotic-sounding combination of rice, fresh vegetables and dairy produce is an almost perfect balance of nutrients and vitamins for your baby.

The dish is best eaten fresh but can be re-heated in the oven or microwave. Younger children will enjoy it liquidized or partially liquidized.

1 Place the boiling water, rice, tomato and onion, if using, in a small saucepan and bring to the boil, then simmer for about 10 minutes.

2 Add the spinach and continue to simmer for another 4 minutes or until the rice is tender – all of the water should have been absorbed. Stir in the cheese and cream cheese or fromage frais and serve immediately.

Serves 1 very small person

Baby Hummus

50 g (2 oz) cooked chickpeas (see below)

3 teaspoons tahini

½ teaspoon lemon juice

2 teaspoons extra virgin olive oil

2½ tablespoons chickpea water or ordinary boiled water

¼ teaspoon chopped garlic (optional)

It is best to make this when you are making hummus for the rest of the family. It freezes well so you can freeze several portions for the baby at the same time.

To prepare the chickpeas, soak them overnight, drain then cook in fresh water for about 1½ hours or until very tender; drain.

1 Place the cooked chickpeas with the rest of the ingredients in a liquidizer or food processor and blend to a smooth paste.

2 Serve accompanied by freshly cut cucumber sticks if your baby is old enough – otherwise serve the hummus on its own.

Serves 1 very small person

Fresh Nectarine Fromage Frais

1 ripe nectarine, peeled, halved and stoned

3 tablespoons fromage frais

Strawberries may be out for tiny babies but fresh ripe nectarines are definitely in. Use only ripe undamaged fruits.

1 Mash the fruit with a fork or purée it in a liquidizer or food processor. Stir into the fromage frais and serve.

Serves 1 tiny person

Field Mushroom Fondue

25 g (1 oz) butter

2 shallots, finely chopped

175 g (6 oz) field mushrooms, roughly chopped

300 ml (½ pint) white grape juice or apple juice

3 teaspoons cornflour

500 g (1 lb) vegetarian mild Cheddar cheese, grated (adults may enjoy Gruyère, Emmental or Jarlsberg)

½ teaspoon dried English mustard

fine sea salt and freshly ground black pepper

½ loaf of soft unbleached white or organic wholewheat bread, cut into cubes

Rather an exotic dish for baby you might say - this dish will happily feed 2 adults and several children so for small families halve the quantities. It will probably be more appreciated by older babies who can get their gums around chunks of bread dipped into the cheese and mushroom mixture. For adults only substitute white grape juice with white wine and add lots of garlic and some chopped basil leaves at the end.

1 Melt the butter in a heavy saucepan, add the shallots and cook until softening. Then stir in the mushrooms and cook for 3 more minutes. Blend a little grape juice with the cornflour.

2 Add the rest of the grape juice to the mushrooms, bring to the boil and reduce by half. Stir in the cornflour and when the mixture has thickened add the cheese, mustard and salt and pepper to taste.

3 Dip in chunks of bread and set a few aside to cool.

Serves 4

SCHOOL DAYS

They say that school days are the 'most happiest days of your life', although it is generally said retrospectively. Nevertheless it is true, but can really only be put into perspective in hindsight. Little do we know when we leave school that things are going to get worse!

With two or more children at school the days simply rocket past so that there is scarcely time to breathe let alone cook, talk, relax or even plan. But plan you must, especially meals, otherwise life will turn into an unending treadmill where food is, at best boring and at worst positively bad for you and your children. Remember once children go to school their appetites immediately double and you are no longer in charge of their tastebuds. This is potentially a very serious state of affairs. I do believe that a lot of petty crime, vandalism and hooliganism stems from the poor diet of a lot of young people today. In many cases it is because both parents have to work, but in lots of cases it is simply down to lack of planning, motivation and know-how on the part of the parents. Cooking for your family, it seems, is no longer considered a priority and in some families it seems impossible. Problems often arise because the male in the family can't or won't cook. More than ever before, all the family members should be made aware of the differences between healthy food and rubbish and family participation in the preparation of meals is essential.

SCHOOL DAY BREAKFASTS

Breakfast is the most important meal of the day, but when everyone is rushing off to school and work it can be a nightmare with many families settling on cereal or toast as their 'kickstart' to the day. There's nothing wrong with cereal or toast as they can be highly nutritious. Cereals should be as natural as possible with no added sugar. Bran flakes or wheat flakes are excellent examples and, like wholemeal toast, should be organic. Toast should be spread with a little unsalted butter and topped with sugar-free jam or suitable savoury spreads. If you like milk with your cereal make sure that the children have full-fat milk even if you prefer skimmed milk yourself. I was spoilt by my mother who, despite having three children, found time to cook each of us exactly what we wanted every morning which sometimes meant cooking eggs in three different ways! The breakfast recipes in this chapter are chosen for speed combined with taste and nutritious content – the sort of meals you can prepare and put on the table in a maximum of 20 minutes.

Egg-Stra Bread

8 slices of your favourite loaf, 3.5 cm (1½ inches) thick, cut diagonally and with 'pocket' formed (see below)

250 g (8 oz) cream cheese

150 g (5 oz) peanut butter, at room temperature

4 ripe bananas, sliced

8 eggs, beaten

350 ml (12 fl oz) milk

½ teaspoon vanilla extract (optional)

½ teaspoon salt

2 tablespoons sesame seeds

125 g (4 oz) butter

This is quick and easy to prepare, very nourishing and fun, too. There's no need to buy special ingredients – unless you want to! Egg-stra bread can be wholesomely savoury or stunningly sweet depending on your mood and your family's preference. The concept is simple, take a thick slice, of your favourite bread – day-old bread is best and cut it in half diagonally. With a knife cut a pocket into the bread along the length of the diagonal being careful not to cut

through the crust. This is filled with your favourite filling, soaked in a mixture of egg and milk and then fried. Egg-stra Bread can be prepared the night before and left soaking in the egg mixture overnight, if you're very short of time.

1 Spoon the cream cheese and peanut butter into the bread 'pockets'. Slip the bananas in with your fingers, making sure the pockets are evenly filled.

2 In a bowl beat the eggs, milk, vanilla extract and salt. Add the bread 'pockets' and let them soak for 2½ minutes on each side, then dip in sesame seeds to coat all over.

3 Heat 25 g (1 oz) of the butter in a frying pan and fry the bread on both sides until golden brown. Keep the 'pockets' warm in the oven while you fry the rest, using the rest of the butter as necessary. Serve, dusted with a little icing sugar or fructose, if liked.

Serves 4

Variations:
With cream cheese – try jam, puréed compôte and fruit.
With grated Cheddar cheese – try cooked mushrooms, raw tomatoes and fresh herbs, roasted peppers, pickles and chutneys.
With peanut butter, try tahini, miso or tofu.

Fruitfast

2 ripe sharontes, honeydew or galia melons, halved and deseeded
250 g (8 oz) fresh raspberries
juice of 1 orange
300 ml (½ pint) Greek yogurt or crème fraîche
1 tablespoon wheatgerm
1 tablespoon clear honey

A fruitfast, not surprisingly, centres breakfast around fresh vitamin-packed fruit. From a health point of view, probably the best thing to enter your stomach after the forced fast of sleep is fruit. Not only does it wake you up, it also wakes up your digestive system in a natural and gentle way, giving you energy and vitamins. Fruitfast takes the nutritional side one step further with its inclusion of wheatgerm and yogurt – both good for us.

Fruitfasts should be made literally just before eating.

1 Place the melon halves on 4 plates. Fill them with the fresh raspberries and douse them in the freshly squeezed orange juice. Top with the Greek yogurt or crème fraîche, sprinkle with wheatgerm and trickle over some honey.

Serves 4

Scrambled Skins

2 large baking potatoes, scrubbed
a little vegetable oil or melted butter
4 free-range eggs (or 6 if not using cream)
150 ml (¼ pint) double or single cream, or milk
fine sea salt
grated vegetarian Cheddar or mozzarella cheese
   (optional)
chopped fresh chives or basil (optional)

Sometimes a slight change in the way you present food can make all the difference as to whether your children will eat it or not. For some reason and despite the fact that baked potatoes are healthy and nutritious most children actually enjoy them. Filled with creamy scrambled eggs they make a quick and easy breakfast that will definitely become a favourite.

1 The night before, prick the potatoes, place in a preheated oven, 200°C (400°F), Gas Mark 6, and bake until they are tender, about 1-1¼ hours. When cooked hollow them out, leaving a reasonably substantial shell. (Keep the potato to use later, perhaps for making bubble and squeak to serve with the Scrambled Skins.) Wrap each potato shell in foil and refrigerate.

2 Next morning brush the skins inside and out with a little vegetable oil or melted butter. Place them in a preheated oven, 200°C (400°F), Gas Mark 6, and let them cook to golden and crispy, about 20 minutes.

3 Meanwhile, slowly cook the scrambled eggs, they'll take about 20-30 minutes using the following technique. Try this recipe at least once; it belies the myth that scrambled eggs should be beaten and actually cooks them without butter or oil.

4 Break the eggs into a cast-iron saucepan. Add the cream or milk and stir the two gently until well blended. Introduce heat to the pan slowly and gently, stirring only occasionally. Avoid letting the mixture boil and season only just before serving. Add the cheese and herbs, if using.

5 Pile the eggs into the potato skins and serve immediately.

Variations:

Scrambled eggs can be the medium to convey many good things into your children's stomachs. Just stir almost anything you fancy into the egg mixture in the latter part of the cooking procedure. Some ingredients will have to be precooked and some are fine added just as they are. The variations are endless; here are some suggestions:

Almost any dairy produce you enjoy, such as cream, cream cheese, natural yogurt, crème fraîche, soured cream, fromage frais, blue cheeses or hard cheeses can be added.

Try adding vegetables such as spinach, onions, tomatoes, peppers and aubergines, mushrooms or asparagus tips.

Apple and Raisin Porridge

125 g (4 oz) barley flakes
125 g (4 oz) jumbo oats
250 g (8 oz) regular oats
4 tablespoons raisins
1 litre (1¾ pints) apple juice
2 apples, peeled, cored and chopped
400 ml (14 fl oz) milk
½ teaspoon ground cinnamon

Porridge can be made from any flaked grain, meal or flour and you can use a mixture of cereals. All of these cereals are best if soaked in their future cooking liquid overnight – not only does this make the cereal more digestible but it also speeds up the cooking time.

1 Soak the barley flakes, all of the oats and the raisins in the apple juice overnight.

2 Place in a large saucepan, add the apples, the milk and the cinnamon and bring to the boil. Simmer, stirring frequently, for 15-20 minutes or until the oats are cooked.

3 Serve the porridge with more milk or yogurt or cream and a little honey to sweeten, if liked.

Serves 4

Big Breakfast Bran Bars

a little oil, for oiling
150 g (5 oz) organic regular oats
150 g (5 oz) organic wholewheat flour
175 ml (6 fl oz) apple juice
25 g (1 oz) wheatgerm
25 g (1 oz) oat bran
125 g (4 oz) raisins
½ teaspoon ground cinnamon
75 g (3 oz) demerara sugar
1 tablespoon molasses (optional)
50 g (2 oz) sesame seeds
125 g (4 oz) chopped mixed nuts
75 ml (3 fl oz) soya oil

This is emergency breakfast material when the children have suddenly discovered homework they had to do or piano they had to practise or perhaps you just got up late. Despite being made of breakfast-type foods they are good at any time of the day and should be made at least weekly and stored in a sealed box or bag in the refrigerator.

1 Grease a 25 x 30 cm (10 x 12 inch) baking tin and line with greaseproof paper.

2 Combine all of the ingredients in a large bowl and mix thoroughly with a wooden spoon. Pour into the prepared tin making sure the mixture reaches right into the corners. Avoid pressing the mixture down to avoid making a solid 'concrete' breakfast bar.

3 Bake in a preheated oven 180°C (350°F), Gas Mark 4, for about 45 minutes, until golden brown. Cut into squares or rectangles while still hot but don't attempt to remove from the tin until they are totally cool.

Serves 4

Peach Blintzes with Loganberry Sauce

PANCAKE BATTER:

3 free-range eggs, beaten

150 g (4 oz) organic wholewheat flour

250 ml (8 fl oz) water or milk, or both

½ teaspoon clear honey or maple syrup

about 1 tablespoon butter, for frying

LOGANBERRY SAUCE:

250 g (8 oz) fresh loganberries

1 teaspoon clear honey

1 drop vanilla extract

1 teaspoon arrowroot

50 ml (2 fl oz) water

PEACH FILLING:

3 sweet, juicy peaches, skinned,
    stoned and sliced

25 g (1 oz) unsalted butter

juice of ½ a lemon

1 tablespoon clear honey

25 g (1 oz) sultanas

¼ teaspoon ground mace

Apart from wondering 'What on earth are 'Blintzes'?' I bet you're thinking 'He's mad'. Blintzes are filled pancakes and, yes, I am suggesting that you have them for breakfast. In actual fact pancakes can take less time to make than omelettes especially if you make the pancake mix the night before. Pancake batter improves with age – up to 24 hours – because the particles of flour start to break down in the egg/milk/water mix making it a smoother batter.

So we've now established that pancakes simply served with lemon and honey or maple syrup are easy; filling them does not take much more effort, either. It's just a question of quickly sautéing some succulent fruit or vegetables in butter and perhaps

a little lemon or orange juice. Blintzes can be sweet or savoury and sweet blintzes can also have a sauce, which is quick to make. I would suggest definitely making the sauce the day before or freezing several sauces from time to time when fresh fruits are in season. And when its all done – watch the children wolf them down. Here's a delicious recipe for fruity blintzes that will make a summer's day shine for sure.

1 Make the batter by blending the eggs, flour, water or milk and honey or syrup together in a bowl to form a smooth creamy liquid. This must be done at least 30 minutes before the pancakes are cooked. If you have made the batter the night before, give it a quick whisk in the morning before using as it will have 'settled out' overnight. The batter must be refrigerated when it is not being used.

2 For the loganberry sauce, heat the loganberries gently in a saucepan with the honey and vanilla. Blend the arrowroot with the water and when the loganberries are boiling fold it in. Alternatively simply pass the loganberries through a sieve to make a delicious coulis. This sauce can be frozen or kept in the refrigerator overnight.

3 To make the filling, stir-fry the peach slices in the gently bubbling butter for 3 minutes. Add the rest of the ingredients and remove from the heat.

4 Melt a little butter in a 20-23 cm (8-9 inch) frying pan or crêpe pan. Add about 4 tablespoons of the pancake batter and cook the pancake for about 1 minute on each side. Continue in this way until all the batter has been used up, keeping the pancakes warm in the oven until ready to use.

5 When ready to serve, place a little peach filling on each pancake, roll up carefully and serve immediately, topped with the warmed loganberry sauce.

Serves 4

Variations:

Try different combinations of fillings and sauces, banana and chocolate, apple and blackberry or strawberry and rhubarb. Try a savoury filling like cheese and mushrooms or baked beans.

Nutty Banana Muffins

175 g (6 oz) coarse unsalted, sugar-free cashew
  nut butter

2 large bananas, mashed

200 ml (7 fl oz) natural yogurt

3 tablespoons clear honey

2 free-range eggs

150 g (5 oz) organic wholewheat flour, sifted

25 g (1 oz) soya flour, sifted

1 teaspoon ground cinnamon

1 teaspoon baking powder

1 teaspoon bicarbonate of soda

25 g (1 oz) sunflower seeds, toasted

a tablespoon butter or vegetable oil, for greasing

50 ml (2 fl oz) unsweetened jam

25 g (1 oz) cashew nut pieces, for decoration

Muffins are a great way to start the day; they are quick, easy to make and versatile. Hot muffins straight from the oven are good on their own or with jam and butter.

Muffins can be baked earlier, frozen and re-heated, wrapped in foil, when required. You can freeze the uncooked mixture in the muffin tins or paper cases and when you want to cook them, add 10 minutes on to the cooking time. Alternatively keep the batter in the refrigerator and use what you need as you need it. The batter will keep for up to 5 days but the lift you get will diminish with age. The most important thing with any muffin is quality of ingredients – so get muffin-making.

1 Mix the cashew nut butter, the bananas, yogurt, honey and eggs together in a bowl. In another bowl combine the flours, cinnamon, baking powder and bicarbonate of soda. Combine the wet and the dry ingredients, then stir in the sunflower seeds.

2 Grease 12 muffin tins. Pour enough mixture into each tin to half fill, add a teaspoon of jam then fill to the top with more muffin mixture.

3 Sprinkle the muffins with cashew pieces then bake them in a preheated oven, 200°C (400°F), Gas Mark 6, for about 25 minutes or until golden brown.

Serves 12 (or 36 tiny ones)

Pear and Plum Compôte

250 g (8 oz) dried pears, soaked overnight in warm
  water with a little vanilla extract, and 125 ml
  (4 fl oz) of the soaking water reserved

375 g (12 oz) Switzen plums, pitted

125 ml (4 fl oz) maple syrup

½ stick of cinnamon

a little grated lemon rind

2 tablespoons lemon juice

juice of 1 orange

Compôtes can always be made in advance ready to be eaten at any time. Make a large batch and keep in the refrigerator. If you've made it right it won't be there long! Compôtes are wonderful healthy foods that are good on their own or on top of, for example, cereal. I like them best served with a good dollop of Greek yogurt or soured cream.

1 Place all of the ingredients together in a large pan. Heat gently, stirring occasionally, until the fruits are soft, about 20-25 minutes. Allow to cool then cover and refrigerate.

2 Served the compôte cold with a heavy and creamy accompaniment such as cream, soured cream, Greek yogurt, fromage frais or crème fraîche.

Serves 4

PACKED LUNCHES, SNACKS AND TEATIME TREATS

For children who don't eat school dinners, packed lunches are vitally important, although, having made sure that they have good breakfasts and dinners, snack lunches can be sufficient. There is virtually no control over what is brought to school in the lunch box and all too often 'one-up-manship' leads to a child having to have a shop-bought chocolate bar included so as to be the same as his or her friend. There is no need for schools to stretch limited budgets by buying meat and meat substitutes like TVP (Textured Vegetable Protein), when with more care and attention they could feed children more healthily and effectively with fresh vegetables, fruits, dairy produce and the vast selection of grains, beans, pulses, seeds, nuts and pastas available today. If the meal looks and tastes good then the children – certainly most children – will eat it. Indeed, increasingly at schools where there is a vegetarian option children are choosing this option because it looks and smells more exciting.

Quite simply your child's packed lunch has to be good. Take for example the standard lunch box – a sandwich, a bag of crisps, a chocolate bar, a piece of fresh fruit and a drink. We will look at each of these items in a little more detail and suggest some healthy alternatives.

When school is over and the children are home the first thing they want is something to eat. It can't be too big or it would spoil their appetite for supper; it's likely to be small, tasty and probably sweet – homemade biscuits or cakes are ideal, or some fruit, cut up if necessary. And then to supper or teatime, your child's main evening meal. Children's friends can be involved at short notice so meals must be flexible, easy to bulk out and occasionally a treat. Day-to-day family suppers generally centre around pasta, pastry, potatoes and bread. Make the dishes elaborate or simple, depending on money, mood and time.

SANDWICHES

First and foremost the sandwich needs good bread. Other considerations must be how to fill it, does it need to travel and should it be served hot? Here are a few ideas that you can use for a packed lunch, a snack or a teatime treat. All of these recipes are suitable for five-year-olds upwards!

To return to bread, there is no point in buying wholewheat bread unless it is made with organic flour. The pesticides used to spray wheat reside in the husk only, so if it's not organic bread buy unbleached white bread. Unless you're toasting it, the bread must be as fresh as can be. In France bakers make bread twice daily, often three times a day because the French people have never accepted that bread should be more than 4 hours old at the time of eating. Sandwiches in packed lunches need to be less messy than those eaten at home, firstly because they have to travel and secondly, because it avoids your child coming home with, for example, great splashes of mayonnaise all over their school uniform. Here are some delicious but not too messy fillings for sandwiches.

Herby Cream Cheese Spread

50 g (2 oz) full-fat cream cheese

75 g (3 oz) butter, melted

2 garlic cloves, crushed, or ½ bunch of spring
  onions, chopped (optional)

1 tablespoon snipped fresh chives

½ tablespoon chopped fresh parsley

½ tablespoon chopped fresh chervil

fine sea salt and freshly ground black pepper

This filling needs no extra butter on the bread and is ideal with cucumbers, tomatoes, onions and almost any salad vegetable or leaf. Try it with nuts or bananas, too.

1 Place the cream cheese in a bowl. Beat the cooled melted butter into it quickly. Add the rest of the ingredients and season. Set aside in the refrigerator until required.

Makes 500 g (1 lb)

Note:

To soften the spread add a little milk, yogurt or cream.

Avocado and Tomato Dip

2 large ripe avocados

2 spring onions, finely chopped

1 large tomato, skinned and chopped

juice of 1 lime

a little chopped coriander, to taste (optional)

1 garlic clove (optional)

¼ teaspoon chilli powder (optional)

fine sea salt and freshly ground black pepper

This has to be made fresh as avocados oxidize quickly, but goes well with salad vegetables, particularly sprouted seeds. You could even combine it with refried beans in a soft flour tortilla (see page 128) to really set the pace at break time. Failing tortillas, use pitta bread or taco shells.

1 Mash the avocados in a bowl and mix in the remaining ingredients, combining well – do not blend or purée the mixture. Use immediately.

Enough for 4 sandwiches

Mushroom 'Spread'

125 g (4 oz) butter

4 shallots, finely chopped

1 kg (2 lb) field mushrooms, finely chopped

250 g (8 oz) butter beans, cooked

2 tablespoons lemon juice

fine sea salt and freshly ground black pepper

Another versatile and natural 'spread' to have around if your children like mushrooms. It is good in sandwiches (hot or cold), choux pastry, tarts and pies.

1 Melt the butter in a pan. Add the shallots and cook until beginning to soften. Add the mushrooms, cover and cook very gently until very soft, as long as you can – preferably about 1½ hours. If there is a lot of liquid, remove the lid after 1 hour and let it evaporate.

2 Place the mushrooms when cool in a liquidizer or food processor. Add the butter beans and lemon juice and purée to a spread-like consistency. Season to taste.

Makes lots

Hummus

250 g (8 oz) chickpeas

1 tablespoon tahini

1 teaspoon ground cumin

3 cloves garlic, crushed

juice of 1 lemon

4 tablespoons extra virgin olive oil

pinch of paprika (optional)

fine sea salt and freshly ground black pepper

Hu.mmous is another firm favourite with the children. It will keep well in the refrigerator for up to 2 weeks - or you can freeze it. It is full of goodness and goes well with all the salad vegetables.

1 Soak the chickpeas overnight.

2 Drain the chickpeas well, then cook in fresh water for about 1½ hours or until they are very tender. Remove from the cooking liquor.

3 Put the remaining ingredients in a blender or food processor and blend together before adding the chickpeas. Add the chickpeas and mix well. If the mixture is too stiff add a little of the chickpea water until it is the right consistency.

Makes lots

Crunchy Egg Spread

4 free-range eggs, hard-boiled (see below)

1 small pepper, cored, deseeded and finely diced

1 stick of celery, finely chopped

3 spring onions, finely chopped

4 gherkins, finely chopped (optional)

1 garlic clove, crushed

1 teaspoon capers, finely chopped

1 teaspoon mustard powder

300 ml (½ pint) good-quality mayonnaise

fine sea salt and freshly ground black pepper

To hard-boil an egg while retaining its flavour and nutritional value is a simple but under-practised art. Carefully place a size 1 egg in a saucepan and cover it with cold water. Bring to the boil, turn off the heat and let the egg sit in the hot water for 6 minutes, then tip out the water and replace with cold water. Smaller eggs require less time. Shell the egg but only slice it when ready to use or eat.

1 Place all of the ingredients in a bowl and mash together with a fork. Adjust the seasoning to taste. Use the spread in sandwiches, together with mustard and cress, if liked.

Enough for 4 sandwiches

ALTERNATIVES TO SANDWICHES

Sandwiches needn't mean just two slices of ordinary bread with something in between. There is a vast array of alternatives, all of which demand their own exciting fillings. Choose from croissants, scones, speciality breads such as focaccia, pitta bread, naan bread and tortillas. Here are just a few ideas; all of which are equally good combined with the basic spreads on pages 81-82.

Cress and Cream Cheese Croissant

2 fresh croissants
125 g (4 oz) cream cheese or a herby cream
   cheese spread
1 punnet of mustard and cress

A decent croissant needs no extra butter. Try filling croissants and serving them cold for a lunch box or serve hot at home.
1 Split the croissants in two and spread cream cheese thickly on each bottom half, pile on the mustard and cress and replace the top half of the croissant. Wrap in aluminium foil for transporting in a lunch box.
Makes 2

Alternative fillings:
If your child likes Brie try a little with redcurrant jelly, mayonnaise and lettuce.

   Use pâtés such as Walnut and Cream Cheese Pâté (see page 20) with a salad garnish, or fill croissants with mozzarella cheese, tomato and a herby mayonnaise.

Savoury Cheese Scones

75 g (3 oz) cream cheese
250 g (8 oz) unbleached plain white flour
1½ teaspoons baking powder
½ teaspoon salt
1 garlic clove, crushed
2 teaspoons finely chopped fresh mixed herbs
1 teaspoon dried mixed herbs
150 ml (¼ pint) milk
beaten egg or milk, for glazing
50 g (2 oz) grated cheese, for topping

Scones are often overlooked as alternative sandwich casings. These scones can be frozen uncooked, then popped in the oven as and when you want them. Serve split in half and buttered, or filled with a pâté or Mushroom Spread (see page 82), topped with a dollop of mango chutney and a salad garnish.
1 In a large bowl rub the cream cheese into the flour, baking powder, salt, garlic and herbs with your fingertips until the mixture resembles fine breadcrumbs.
2 Quickly stir in the milk to form a soft dough and shape it into a ball with floured hands.
3 On a lightly floured surface gently roll out the dough to a thick-

Overleaf Left- HUMMUS, PAI N BAGNAT, CRESS AND CREAM CHEESE CROISSANT *Right-* CRUDITES, AVOCADO AND TOMATO DIP, SAVOURY CHEESE SCONES, PAIN BAGNAT.

ness of 2.5 cm (1 inch) and cut out the scones using a 5 cm (2 inch) cutter.

4 Brush the tops with egg or milk to glaze and sprinkle with grated cheese. Place on a lightly greased baking sheet and bake in a preheated oven, 220°C (425°F), Gas Mark 7, for 10-15 minutes or until they are well risen and golden brown.

5 Remove from the oven and serve immediately if you're eating them at home; otherwise allow to cool before filling.

Makes 6

Pain Bagnat (Bathed Bread)

1 large ripe tomato, cut into chunks

½ cucumber, peeled and cut into similar size chunks

1 red pepper, cored, deseeded and cubed (grilled first, if liked)

4 spring onions, chopped

4 leaves of Chinese leaf, chopped

50 g (2 oz) bean sprouts or sprouted seeds

1 tablespoon cashew nuts, toasted

8 black olives, pitted (optional)

4 artichoke hearts, sliced (optional)

125 g (4 oz) vegetarian Cheddar, mozzarella, feta, goats' cheese or tofu

4 crusty organic wholewheat or unbleached white rolls, the tops removed and centres hollowed out

TOMATO AND BASIL VINAIGRETTE:

3 teaspoons Dijon mustard

1 tablespoon tomato purée

25 g (1 oz) basil leaves, torn into pieces

3 tablespoons white wine vinegar

1 dessertspoon demerara sugar

2 garlic cloves, crushed (optional)

300 ml (½ pint) extra virgin olive oil

fine sea salt and freshly ground black pepper

Originating in southern France, this is my sort of food: a crusty bread roll which becomes a 'container' for a salad. The hard bread 'shell' soaks up any excess dressing. Try spooning some of the Mushroom Spread (see page 82), Walnut and Cream Cheese Pâté (see page 20) or hummus into the roll before adding the salad and dressing.

1 For the vinaigrette dressing, whisk all the ingredients except the oil together in a jug. Gradually add the oil, whisking all the time. Season to taste.

2 Mix all the salad ingredients and then spoon them into the hollowed out rolls. Cover with the vinaigrette and then replace the lids. Serve immediately.

Makes 4

Variations:

Try adding favourite marinated vegetables such as mushrooms, aubergines and courgettes or pickled onions, gherkins and cauliflower. Avocado and cooked beetroot are delicious, too.

Try other salad leaves such as chicory, gem lettuce or rocket.

HOT SANDWICHES

The following recipes are no good for packed lunches but make great snacks at home. All you need is a grill and an excellent imagination. Keep planning to a bare minimum - use up what's in your refrigerator and store cupboard.

Croque Enfant

8 large slices of unbleached white bread

1 tablespoon French mustard

125 g (4 oz) brown mushrooms, sautéed in butter

1 bunch of chives, snipped

125 g (4 oz) Edam, Emmental or Gruyère cheese,
    freshly grated

125 g (4 oz) softened butter

In France the only hot sandwiches are Croque Monsieur (bland béchamel and slimy ham and Croque Madame (bland béchamel with a frankfurter). No great sandwich has developed in France because on the whole they do not recognise a need for a quick snack – a meal is a meal and lasts for at least 2 hours. So here is my alternative – Croque Enfant – a grilled open sandwich that most children will love as a snack or for supper.

1 Put the slices of bread on a work surface, spread with some mustard and top with the sautéed mushrooms. Sprinkle with the chives. Cover the mushrooms evenly with the grated cheese. Put the remaining slices of bread on top.

2 Butter the outside of the sandwiches and place on a baking sheet. Bake in a preheated oven, 220°C (425°F), Gas Mark 7, for about 5 minutes or until crispy and golden on both sides. Alternatively cook in a sandwich toaster.

Makes 4

Variations:

Substitute grilled or sautéed vegetables such as peppers, tomatoes, aubergines or onions for the mushrooms. For a nutritious vegan sandwich, replace the cheese with grilled marinated tofu.

Gruyère and Tomato Toasts

2 garlic cloves, crushed (optional)

2 tablespoons extra virgin olive oil

1 baguette, cut diagonally into 12 x 1 cm (½ inch)
    thick slices

4 vine-ripened fresh plump tomatoes, each cut into 3

175 g (6 oz) Gruyère or vegetarian Cheddar cheese,
    grated, or sliced into 15 g (½ oz) portions

fine sea salt and freshly ground black pepper

basil leaves, torn into small pieces, to garnish

1 Mix the garlic, if using with the olive oil and brush one side of each baguette slice with it. Toast both sides of the bread under a grill until lightly browned. If necessary brush a little more oil on the oiled sides of the bread. Top each with tomato, season, then top with cheese and season again.

2 Place on an oiled baking sheet and cook in a preheated oven, 190°C (375°F), Gas Mark 5, or under the grill for 6-8 minutes until the cheese is bubbling. Sprinkle with basil and serve.

Makes 12

Variations:

Use mozzarella or goats' cheese. Substitute peppers, aubergines, onions or mushrooms for the tomatoes. Top with sun-dried tomatoes or peppers in olive oil.

Overleaf Left- GRUYÈRE AND TOMATO TOASTS, HEY PRESTO PIZZA, CHEESY CORN AND MUSHROOM MUFFINS *Right-* GRUYÈRE AND TOMATO TOASTS, CHEESY CORN AND MUSHROOM MUFFINS

Cheesy Corn and Mushroom Muffins

25 g (1 oz) butter, plus extra for greasing

1 small leek, white part only, finely chopped

125 g (4 oz) open cup mushrooms

75 g (3 oz) organic wholewheat flour

125 ml (4 fl oz) milk or water

50 g (2 oz) vegetarian Cheddar cheese, grated

250 g (8 oz) frozen or drained, canned sweetcorn

2 free-range eggs, beaten

25 g (1 oz) wheatgerm

25 g (1 oz) cornmeal

1 teaspoon dried oregano

2 teaspoons baking powder

1 teaspoon bicarbonate of soda

fine sea salt and freshly ground black pepper

To garnish:

a little grated cheese

sesame seeds

1 Melt the butter in a pan and cook the leeks for about 3 minutes, add the mushrooms and cook for 5 minutes. Stir in 15 g (½ oz) of the flour and cook for about 1 minute.

2 Gradually add the milk to make a sauce, stir in the cheese and the sweetcorn. Set aside.

3 In a bowl combine the eggs, wheatgerm, cornmeal, the remaining flour, oregano, baking powder and bicarbonate of soda. Season lightly.

4 Grease 12 muffin tins with a little butter.

5 Combine the vegetable mixture with the flour mixture and spoon into the muffin tins. Sprinkle the muffins with a little cheese and sesame seeds and bake in a preheated oven, 200°C (400°F), Gas Mark 6, for 20 minutes. Serve as a snack or with steamed vegetables as a meal.

Makes 12

Welsh Crumpet

40 g (1½ oz) butter

40 g (1½ oz) organic wholewheat flour

200 ml (7 fl oz) brown ale

275 g (9 oz) Cheshire cheese, grated

1 large tablespoon prepared English mustard

1 garlic clove, crushed (optional)

8 crumpets

fine sea salt and freshly ground black pepper

This is a variation of Welsh Rarebit – crumpets are in fact of Welsh origin, too. Serve 2 crumpets per child and 4 for adults. They are ideal for teatime.

1 Make the sauce by melting the butter in a small pan and whisking in the flour until well combined. Gradually add the beer, whisking continuously to make a thick sauce. Stir in the grated cheese and mustard, season to taste and add the crushed garlic, if using.

2 Place the crumpets upside down under a preheated grill and grill until lightly browned. Remove from the grill, turn over and top with a spoonful of the cheese sauce. Put them back under the grill until they are golden brown.

Makes 8

Variation:

Top the crumpets with tomato, cooked onion or mushrooms prior to adding the cheese sauce.

Hey Presto Pizza

4 x 15 cm (6 inch) focaccia (plain olive oil or onion
  flavour is excellent)
1 tablespoon olive oil
2 garlic cloves, crushed
1 large onion, finely sliced
1 red pepper, cored, deseeded and finely sliced
1 tablespoon tomato purée
6 tomatoes, sliced
125 g (4 oz) mozzarella or vegetarian Cheddar cheese,
  or a mixture of the two, grated
3 teaspoons dried basil
fine sea salt and freshly ground black pepper

*Just about every child in the world likes pizzas and since they are
so easy to make at home I don't understand why people buy
them. O.K. you buy them to save time, but they don't take any
time anyway. If you want a ready-made base don't go for the
vacuum-packed bases when virtually every baker or supermarket
now stocks focaccia. This Italian flat bread is one of the origins of
pizza and the moist dough, rich with olive oil, re-heats beautifully. So just top an individual focaccia or a large one with your
favourite topping and away you go.*

1 Place the focaccia on a well-oiled baking sheet.

2 Heat the olive oil in a small heavy frying pan. Add the garlic and
cook for a few minutes. Add the onion and pepper and cook for
another 2 minutes.

3 Spread a little tomato purée on to each focaccia. Top with the
tomato slices and pile the cooked onions, garlic and peppers on to
the top.

4 Mix the grated cheese with the basil and seasoning and sprinkle
over the pizzas. Place in a preheated oven, 220°C (425°F), Gas
Mark 7, and bake for 15-20 minutes until golden brown. Serve
with a crisp salad.

Makes 4

'Sausage' Rolls

2 tablespoons vegetable oil
1 onion, finely chopped
1 stick of celery, finely chopped
2 teaspoons dried thyme
125 g (4 oz) flat mushrooms, finely chopped
175 g (6 oz) red lentils
300 ml (½ pint) water
1 tablespoon tomato purée
2 tablespoons peanut butter
1 tablespoon shoyu
1 garlic clove, crushed (optional)
75 g (3 oz) wholewheat breadcrumbs
500 g (1 lb) puff pastry, thawed if frozen
fine sea salt and freshly ground black pepper
beaten egg, to glaze
1 tablespoon sesame seeds, to decorate

Our sausage rolls are without meat and will appeal to everyone.

1 Heat the oil in a pan, cook the onion, celery and thyme until
beginning to soften. Add the mushrooms and lentils and cook for
2 minutes. Stir in the water, tomato purée, peanut butter, shoyu
and garlic. Cover and cook gently for 20 minutes.

2 Fold in the breadcrumbs and season, set aside to cool. If the
mixture is very chunky purée half of it in a liquidizer or food
processor then return to the remaining mixture and mix together.

3 On a lightly floured surface, roll out the pastry to a 15 x 60 cm
(6 x 24 inch) rectangle. Spoon the filling down the centre of the
rectangle, moisten one long edge of the pastry and fold over. Seal
by crimping or by hand.

5 Brush with beaten egg yolk and sprinkle with sesame seeds.
Cut across into 20 small or 10 big rolls. Refrigerate for 30 minutes
prior to cooking. Bake in a preheated oven, 220°C (425°F), Gas
Mark 7, for 25 minutes until well risen and golden brown.

Makes 36

Empanadas

1 tablespoon extra virgin olive oil

½ teaspoon chilli powder

½ teaspoon ground cumin

1 onion, finely chopped

1 garlic clove, crushed

125 g (4 oz) chestnut mushrooms, sliced

1 red pepper, cored, deseeded and finely cubed

200 g (7 oz) can sweetcorn, drained

2 large ripe tomatoes, skinned and chopped

½ tablespoon tomato purée

50 g (2 oz) vegetarian Cheddar cheese, grated

50 g (2 oz) mozzarella cheese, grated

¾ quantity of tortilla dough (see Mexican Fajitas
    and Frijoles, page 128)

olive oil, for frying

fine sea salt and freshly ground black pepper

*Empanadas are a Spanish version of English pasties,
Russian piroshkis, Turkish boreks and Indian samosas.
Empanadas were originally made using bread dough. Here
I've suggested using floury tortilla dough (see page 128) but
if this is inconvenient use frozen puff pastry. Empanadas
may be deep-fried, baked or shallow-fried. They are good
hot or cold and make a great supper or a lunch box filler.*

1 To make the filling, heat the oil in a frying pan, stir in the
spices, onion and garlic and sauté until beginning to soften.
Add the mushrooms and peppers and cook for 5 minutes.

2 Stir in the sweetcorn and tomatoes and cook for another
5 minutes before adding the tomato purée and seasoning.
Set aside to cool before folding in the cheeses.

3 To assemble, the dough must be rolled out very thinly so
it is best to prepare it in small pieces. Cut the pastry into
circles with a 7.5 cm (3¼ inch) diameter round cutter.

4 Spoon a little filling into the centre of each circle, dampen
the edges, fold over and crimp together to seal.

5 Fry the empanadas in about 1 cm (½ inch) of hot oil in a
frying pan until golden. Drain on kitchen paper and serve
with a good salsa, salad and potatoes. Alternatively, serve
cold on their own or with pickles.

Serves 4

Spinach and Potato Hash

4 tablespoons extra virgin olive oil

2 onions, cut into wedges

500 g (1 lb) potatoes, very thinly sliced

2 garlic cloves, crushed (optional)

2 teaspoons chopped fresh chives, thyme or parsley

125 g (4 oz) fresh spinach, stalks removed

4 free-range eggs, beaten

50 g (2 oz) mozzarella or vegetarian Cheddar
    cheese, grated

fine sea salt and freshly ground black pepper

*Here is a dish to get vital vitamins down eager young
throats. It's quite simple and versatile, and best made with
leftover vegetables.*

1 Heat the oil in a casserole dish. Add the onions and potatoes, seasoning, garlic and herbs and sauté for 5 minutes
until well coated in oil and the potatoes are starting to
colour. Place the casserole dish in a preheated oven, 200°C
(400°F), Gas Mark 6, for 25 minutes.

2 Remove the dish from the oven and stir in the spinach and
eggs. Sprinkle cheese over the top and return to the oven.
Bake for 10 minutes or until the eggs are set, then serve.

Serves 4

Variation:

*Use shallots instead of onions and replace the spinach
with broccoli or peppers, aubergine or tomatoes.*

ESSENTIALLY SWEET

Of course no packed lunch or teatime treat would be complete without a little something sweet. Anything from a good ripe whole fresh fruit to a homemade chocolate chip cookie falls into this category. These tasty recipes are simple to make and range from a delicious Apple Sauce Cake, tempting Sultana and Peanut Butter Cookies to a mouth-watering Banana Yogurt Cake and Very Fruity Bars.

These treats are particularly robust and are ideal for surviving the rigours of a lunch box or filling that appetite gap children have when they come home from school. They keep well in an airtight tin and are easy to make in bulk; back-up stocks for emergencies, can also be frozen; in most cases.

All too often we are consumed by guilt on biting into something evenly remotely sweet. Most of these recipes use a minimum of natural refined sugars and a maximum of fruit, to reduce that guilty feeling after a wonderful but sinfully rich treat. All children and adults will love them!.

Apple Sauce Cake

CAKE:

125 g (4 oz) unsalted butter

125 g (4 oz) demerara sugar

2 free-range eggs (size 1), beaten

1 teaspoon vanilla extract

½ teaspoon grated orange rind

250 g (8 oz) organic wholewheat flour

3 teaspoons baking powder

½ teaspoon salt

1 teaspoon ground cinnamon

½ teaspoon ground allspice

50 g (2 oz) nuts, chopped

50 g (2 oz) raisins

250 g (8 oz) unsweetened apple purée

TOPPING:

3 tablespoons chopped mixed nuts

25 g (1 oz) butter

50 g (2 oz) organic wholewheat flour

2 tablespoons demerara sugar

½ teaspoon ground cinnamon

This is an extremely appetizing and nutritious cake that keeps well.

1 Cream the butter and the sugar together in a large bowl. Add the eggs gradually then stir in the vanilla extract and orange rind.

2 In another bowl, combine the remaining ingredients – except the apple purée – and fold carefully into the creamed mixture, then stir in the apple purée.

3 Pour into a greased 20 cm (8 inch) round cake tin, levelling the surface. Mix the topping ingredients together and sprinkle over the top. Bake in a preheated oven, 160°C (325°F), Gas Mark 3, for 1½ hours, or until an inserted skewer comes out clean.

4 Remove from the oven and allow the cake to cool in the tin before turning out.

Makes a 20 cm (8 inch) cake

Power Punch

125 g (4 oz) Power Base (see below)

750 ml (1¼ pints) fresh unsweetened orange, apple or
   pineapple juice

2 ripe bananas, peeled and chopped

2 large dessert apples, cored and roughly chopped

25 ml (1 fl oz) natural yogurt

*Quite often there simply isn't much in the cake or biscuit tin and
you don't have time to make anything. 'But I'm starving…' cry
the children.*

*Power Punches consist of seeds, cereals, fruits and dairy pro-
duce (if liked) combined together in a blender to make a smooth,
satisfying and energy-packed liquid refreshment. Don't feel confined to the suggestions in this recipe; just use your own favourite
ingredients. To simplify the procedure first decide on a base then
add to it when the occasion demands. Mainly cereal 'power
bases' like the one listed below can be kept in the refrigerator or
freezer and used from frozen.*

1 Simply blend all the ingredients together in a liquidizer or food
processor until smooth and serve with or without ice.

Serves 4

Power base:

*To make a Power Base, blend all of the following ingredients
together until very fine then store in the refrigerator or freezer.
Use 25 g (1 oz) of Power Base per person.*

25 g (1 oz) cocoa or carob powder

25 g (1 oz) wheatgerm

25 g (1 oz) coarse oatmeal

25 g (1 oz) sunflower seeds

25 g (1 oz) sesame seeds

15 g (½ oz) brewer's yeast, powdered

50 g (2 oz) full-fat milk powder (optional)

25 g (1 oz) unsweetened desiccated coconut

Ultimate Shortcake

125 g (4 oz) organic wholewheat flour

50 g (2 oz) ground almonds

125 g (4 oz) butter

50 g (2 oz) golden caster sugar

½ egg yolk

pinch of salt

fine unsweetened desiccated coconut, for dusting

*Organic wholewheat shortcake can be delicious but once again it
is the ingredients that count. This is a perfect family snack and far
more satisfying than a packet of shop-bought biscuits. With judi-
cious use of fresh fruits and cream you can turn it into a sumptuous dessert.*

1 Mix the flour and the almonds together in a bowl. Add the butter and the sugar and rub in together. Stir in the egg yolk and salt.
Mix well and knead to form a smooth dough.

2 Place a 20 cm (8 inch) flan ring on a lightly greased baking sheet
and press the dough into it. Alternatively, roll the dough out to a
20 cm (8 inch) round if you don't have a flan ring – it will still taste
as good. Lightly mark the shortcake into 8 wedges and then chill
for about 30 minutes.

3 Place in a preheated oven, 160°C (325°F), Gas Mark 3, and
bake for 30 minutes or until pale golden brown. Remove from the
oven, re-score the wedges and dust with fine desiccated coconut.
Allow the shortcake to cool for 5 minutes only on the baking
sheet then lift off carefully using 2 palette knives and place on a
wire rack to complete cooling.

Makes 8

Overleaf Left- BANANA YOGHURT CAKE *Right-* APPLE SAUCE CAKE,
SULTANA AND PEANUT BUTTER COOKIES, VERY FRUITY BARS.

Very Fruity Bars

175 g (6 oz) pitted prunes

175 g (6 oz) whole dried apricots

175 g (6 oz) whole dried bananas, chopped into
   1 cm (½ inch) pieces

125 g (4 oz) raisins

175 g (6 oz) chopped mixed nuts

175 g (6 oz) unsweetened desiccated coconut

125 g (4 oz) organic wholewheat flour

125 g (4 oz) regular oats

75 ml (3 fl oz) soya oil

75 ml (3 fl oz) maple syrup or organic
   apple concentrate

1 teaspoon almond extract

1 teaspoon vanilla extract

50 g (2 oz) sunflower seeds

1 Place the prunes, apricots, bananas and raisins in a large bowl. Pour in enough cold water to cover and leave them to soak overnight.

2 Grease a 25 x 30 cm (10 x 12 inch) baking sheet and line with silicone paper.

3 Mix all of the ingredients together in a bowl. If the mixture seems too dry add a little more liquid from the soaked fruit. Tip the mixture into the prepared tin, gently pressing it into the corners and levelling the surface.

4 Bake for 30 minutes in a preheated oven, 160°C (325°F), Gas Mark 3, or until golden brown. Remove and allow to cool before cutting.

5 Cut the bars into 3 lengthways and into 6 across to make 18 rectangles that will fit nicely into a lunch box or cake tin. These bars keep very well, especially since they contain no dairy produce.

Makes 18

Sultana and Peanut Butter Cookies

2 free-range eggs

125 ml (4 fl oz) milk

50 g (2 oz) unsalted butter

½ teaspoon grated nutmeg

½ teaspoon ground cinnamon

½ teaspoon ground cloves

1 teaspoon vanilla extract

175 g (6 oz) crunchy peanut butter

125 g (4 oz) organic wholewheat flour

50 g (2 oz) soya flour

1 teaspoon baking powder

½ teaspoon salt

25 g (1 oz) wheatgerm

50 g (2 oz) sultanas

These cookies are miniature feasts and combine all the nutrients growing children need as well as being great for adults, too.

1 Place the eggs, milk, butter, spices, vanilla extract and peanut butter in a mixing bowl or food processor and mix together well.

2 In a separate bowl combine all the dry ingredients except the sultanas. Combine the two mixtures together, fold in the sultanas.

3 Line a greased baking sheet with silicone paper and place spoonfuls of the cookie mixture on to the paper, spacing well apart and gently flattening each mound with the back of the spoon. Bake in a preheated oven, 230°C (450°F), Gas Mark 8, for 8-12 minutes until golden brown.

4 Remove from the oven and allow to cool on a wire rack before eating.

Makes 24

Date and Walnut Crunch Cake

BASE:

50 g (2 oz) organic wholewheat flour

25 g (1 oz) soya flour

25 g (1 oz) wheatbran

25 g (1 oz) wheatgerm

2 tablespoons soya oil

25 g (1 oz) unsalted butter or vegan margarine

½ teaspoon vanilla extract

TOPPING:

125 g (4 oz) dried dates, soaked in 125 ml (4 fl oz) warm
   water overnight

1 tablespoon clear honey (optional)

125 g (4 oz) walnuts, chopped

*Make this cake another excellent yet robust addition to your ever-
expanding repertoire.*

1 For the base, mix all the ingredients together in a bowl or blend
in a food processor until they resemble coarse breadcrumbs.

2 Grease a 15 x 25 cm (6 x 10 inch) baking sheet and line with silicone paper. Press three-quarters of the shortbread base mixture
into the tin and bake in a preheated oven, 180°C (350°F), Gas
Mark 4, for 15 minutes.

3 Meanwhile, cook the dates briefly in the water in which they
have been soaking. Stir in the honey, if using, and the chopped
nuts. Spread evenly over the precooked base then top with the
remaining shortbread mixture.

4 Return to the oven and cook for another 10 minutes. Allow to
cool before cutting into 24 pieces.

Makes 24

Variation:

*Substitute figs, prunes or apricots for the dates and adjust the
sweetening accordingly.*

Banana Yogurt Cake

125 ml (4 fl oz) yogurt

175 g (6 oz) demerara sugar

125 g (4 oz) butter, melted, or
   125 ml (4 fl oz) vegetable oil

2 very ripe bananas, mashed

2 free-range eggs, (size 1), beaten

175 g (6 oz) organic wholewheat flour, sifted

1½ teaspoons baking powder

pinch of salt

finely grated rind of 1 lemon

*This is a beautifully moist cake that positively explodes with
goodness. It is good as is, or can be dressed up to look quite fancy
for a special occasion.*

1 Grease a 20 cm (8 inch) cake tin with oil or butter and line with
greaseproof paper.

2 Beat the yogurt and sugar together in a bowl until smooth.
Whisk in the melted butter or vegetable oil quickly, followed by
the bananas and the eggs.

3 In another bowl sift together the flour, baking powder and salt.
Then carefully fold into the egg mixture and stir in the lemon rind.

4 Tip the mixture into the prepared cake tin. Place in a preheated oven, 180°C (350°F) Gas Mark 4, and bake for 45-55 minutes
or until firm to the touch. Turn out on to a wire rack to cool.

Makes a 20 cm (8 inch) cake

Variations:

*This cake is good decorated with fresh summer fruits or
unsweetened jam.*

*Alternatively, top with a wholesome cream cheese and
lemon frosting, made by combining 125 g (4 oz) cream cheese
with the grated rind and juice of ½ lemon or lime and 50 g
(2 oz) light brown sugar. Top with a few strips of lemon or
lime rind to decorate.*

FUNDAMENTAL SUPPERS

These are the core of family life – work – or school day suppers that are the very thread of existence. In most families they must by necessity be quick and easy to prepare and economically viable. If your children are prone to inviting friends back unexpectedly the meals must also be easily extendable. Ideally they should be enjoyed by children and adults alike; adults often tend to eat later than the children so fundamental suppers should be good re-heated or else easy to set aside portions for cooking an hour or two later. Fundamental suppers have no set rules – everything that is cooked has to fit into your time scale. Therefore it is quite probable that dessert will only appear after the simplest of main dishes and equally more complex supper dishes will leave time only for fresh fruit, yogurt or fromage frais for afters.

Picture the situation, " Mum can Charlotte come home for tea?" Have only just got back from work yourself, hastily cobbled together enough macaroni cheese for you and your family and dashed to school to pick up the children. Solution - buy a cauliflower or some mushrooms on your way home. Poach the cauliflower or sauté the mushrooms before adding them into your macaroni cheese. Alternatively knock up a quick and healthy salad to accompany the macaroni. Nine times out of ten an extra mouth to feed at a meal will be no problem unless the meal comes in portions like Bambeano Burgers or stuffed pancakes. In such situations try to cook in batches and have a few spare in the freezer you'll find it invaluable stock for unexpected occasions and guests.

FUNDAMENTAL MAIN COURSES

Pasta, rice, potatoes and bread are probably the fastest 'instant' foods in our kitchen and consequently form the base of many fundamental suppers. There's no reason why a perfectly good meal using the simplest of ingredients cannot be made within 20 minutes using such basic, nourishing and solid foundations.

This chapter includes a few main meal pasta sauces that could equally top rice or potatoes. When using dried pasta, remember to allow 75-125 g (3-4 oz) per person. Boil it in plenty of water, adding salt and oil only if you want to. When the pasta is cooked, season it and serve immediately with a knob of butter or a splosh of good fruity olive oil. If you are cooking the pasta in advance immerse it quickly in cold water and leave under a cold running tap until cold, to stop the pasta sticking together.

Instant Fresh Tomato and Basil Sauce

2 tablespoons extra virgin olive oil

1 large onion, finely sliced

3 garlic cloves, crushed

500 g (1 lb) ripe tomatoes, skinned, deseeded and chopped, the juice retained

20 basil leaves, torn into pieces

a little brown sugar or balsamic vinegar, to taste

fine sea salt and freshly ground black pepper

In almost the time it takes to open and cook a packet of instant tomato sauce this fresh sauce can be made using nature's very own instant ingredients – tomatoes, garlic and basil. Make the sauce while the pasta is cooking.
1 Heat the oil in a frying pan. Add the onions and garlic and cook until beginning to soften. Add the tomatoes and cook for a further 10 minutes. Stir in the basil, season and add sugar or balsamic vinegar to adjust the acidity. Serve with pasta or rice topped with grated Cheddar or Parmesan.
Serves 4

Variations:
Add peppers, mushrooms, sweetcorn, lentils, green beans, olives and even a dollop of soured cream. Try other herbs like marjoram, parsley or chervil.

Instant 'Canned' Tomato and Basil Sauce

2 tablespoons extra virgin olive oil

1 large onion, finely sliced

3 garlic cloves, crushed

1 dessertspoon demerara sugar

1 tablespoon balsamic vinegar, or 2 tablespoons red wine vinegar

1 tablespoon tomato purée

2 x 425 g (14 oz) cans chopped tomatoes

20 basil leaves, torn into pieces

fine sea salt and freshly ground black pepper

Fresh tomatoes are often not what they should be. Picked green and forced to travel, many are barely suitable to use salads, let alone sauces. So here is a recipe using the finest canned Italian plum tomatoes. The trouble with canned tomatoes is of course the metallic flavour. This is easily removed with plenty of cooking but if you want to do it quickly other ingredients must be used, primarily vinegar and honey or sugar.

1 Heat the oil in a large heavy saucepan. Add the onion and garlic and sauté until beginning to soften and darken in colour. Add the sugar and vinegar and reduce by half. Stir in the tomato purée, cook for 1 minute, then add the canned chopped tomatoes.

2 Bring to the boil and partially cover the saucepan to reduce the sauce and prevent your stove or hob from being splattered with tomato juice. After 5 minutes stir in the basil and adjust the seasoning.

3 Allow the tomato sauce to simmer while cooking your pasta or rice.

Serves 4

Indonesian Peanut Sauce

1 tablespoon vegetable oil

1 large onion, finely sliced

½ teaspoon chilli powder

1 teaspoon ground cumin

1 large green pepper, cored, deseeded and cut into small strips

2 garlic cloves, crushed

1 tablespoon demerara sugar

3-4 tablespoons lemon juice

250 g (8 oz) crunchy peanut butter

450 ml (¾ pint) hot water

1 tablespoon shoyu

freshly ground black pepper

This is a really simple peanut sauce that can be adjusted to suit your children's tastebuds. Serve it with Chinese egg noodles, pasta, rice or as a topping for baked potatoes.

1 Heat the oil in large heavy saucepan. Add the onion, spices and a little black pepper and cook gently for 5 minutes. Stir in the green pepper and garlic and cook for a further 5 minutes over a slightly higher heat.

2 Add the sugar and lemon juice, cook for 1 minute, stirring well. Fold in the peanut butter and quickly add the water, stirring to a smooth consistency. Bring to the boil, add the shoyu and adjust the seasoning to taste.

3 Serve the sauce with rice or pasta with raw or steamed vegetables such as cucumber, yellow peppers, Chinese leaf, mangetout, bean sprouts and chopped spring onions; roasted whole peanuts are good here too. Sprinkle with a little finely desiccated coconut or grated cheese, if liked.

Cheesy Spinach and Mushroom Sauce

15 g (½ oz) butter

15 g (½ oz) unbleached plain white flour

300 ml (½ pint) full-fat milk

125 g (4 oz) vegetarian Cheddar cheese, grated

½ teaspoon grated nutmeg

2 teaspoons mustard powder

125 g (4 oz) cherry tomatoes, halved and grilled

125 g (4 oz) mushrooms, thinly sliced

200g (7 oz) fresh spinach, stalks removed

fine sea salt and freshly ground black pepper

Another very quick multi-functional sauce.

1 Melt the butter in a small saucepan and stir in the flour quickly to make a roux, cook for about 1½ minutes. Set aside to cool for 1 minute and bring the milk to the boil in another saucepan.

2 Return the roux to the stove and gradually add the hot milk over a medium to high heat, stirring all the time. As the sauce thickens more liquid can be added without curdling. Add the remaining ingredients, stir and cook for 3 minutes over a low heat until all the spinach has wilted.

3 Adjust the seasoning to taste and serve on a bed of pasta, rice or baked potatoes, topped with grated Cheddar or Parmesan.

Serves 4

Variations:
Crumble in a little blue cheese and add a glass of white wine to the sauce.

Try adding lightly sautéed courgettes, broccoli, leeks, red or green peppers and cauliflower.

Mexican Rice

3 tablespoons extra virgin olive oil

1 large onion, finely chopped

1 red pepper, cored, deseeded and cut into
   1 cm (½ inch) cubes

1 green pepper, cored, deseeded and cut into
   1 cm (½ inch) cubes

125 g (4 oz) button mushrooms, sliced

500 g (1 lb) long-grain brown rice

500 g (1 lb) ripe tomatoes, skinned, deseeded and
   chopped, or 425 g (14 oz) can chopped tomatoes

3 garlic cloves, crushed

½ poblano or ancho chilli

600 ml (1 pint) hot vegetable stock or water

300 ml (½ pint) dry white wine or vegetable stock

125 g (4 oz) fresh or frozen peas

125 g (4 oz) frozen or drained, canned sweetcorn

125 g (4 oz) drained, canned kidney beans (the liquid
   can be used in the stock)

fine sea salt and freshly ground black pepper

2 tablespoons chopped fresh coriander, to garnish

This rice dish is fresh and colourful, including many favourite ingredients. The quantity of chilli given in this recipe will make the dish only slightly spicy, so do adjust it according to your family's taste. Poblano is a fresh chilli, ancho is the dried version with the seeds removed.

Mexican Rice is a complete meal in itself or makes a good side dish for a Mexican dinner party.

1 Heat the olive oil in your largest, heaviest casserole dish. Add the onion and sauté for 5 minutes. Add the peppers and mushrooms and cook for a further 5 minutes before stirring in the rice.

2 Meanwhile, purée together the tomatoes, garlic and chilli in a liquidizer or food processor.

3 When the rice is well coated in oil, stir in the tomato purée and cook for 3 minutes.

4 Bring the stock or water and the wine to the boil and add it gradually to the rice mixture until all of the liquid has been absorbed and the rice is tender, this will take 15-20 minutes. Alternatively, add all of the liquid at once to the rice, stir once then cover and leave for 15 minutes. Cook over a low heat to reduce the risk of burning.

5 Stir in the peas, sweetcorn and kidney beans, cover and allow to finish cooking for 5 minutes. Season to taste and serve the rice garnished with freshly chopped coriander.

Serves 4-6

Leek and Courgette Stir-Fry

2 tablespoons extra virgin olive oil

3 leeks, thinly sliced

2 courgettes, thinly sliced

1 large red pepper, cored, deseeded and
  thinly sliced

500 g (1 lb) cooked pasta or rice

10 basil leaves, torn into pieces

1 tablespoon sesame seeds

1 garlic clove, crushed

½ tablespoon tomato purée

fine sea salt and freshly ground black pepper

*Pasta and rice dishes in particular often need no more than
a quick and tasty stir-fry to turn them into a meal. Simply
put the pasta or rice on to cook – prepare the vegetables and
stir-fry them. More complex stir-fries involving a wide variety of vegetables, nuts and tofu can be added to Chinese
noodles or rice for an oriental feast.*

1 Heat the oil in a large heavy saucepan. Sauté the leeks,
courgettes and red pepper for about 10 minutes over a
medium heat.

2 Add the cooked pasta or rice and continue to fry for
another 3 minutes. Stir in the basil, sesame seeds, garlic and
tomato purée. Season to taste and serve immediately.

Serves 4

Variations:
*Try using onions or shallots, mushrooms, broccoli,
skinned and deseeded tomatoes, carrots, green beans and
nuts. For oriental versions, add Chinese leaf, water
chestnuts, Chinese mushrooms, bean sprouts and
5-spice powder.*

Swiss Soufflé Potatoes

4 large baking potatoes, baked and the flesh
  scooped-out

3 tablespoons finely chopped spring onions

75 g (3 oz) Gruyère cheese, grated

75 g (3 oz) Emmental cheese, grated

2 garlic cloves, crushed

25 g (1 oz) butter

25 g (1 oz) organic wholewheat flour

150 ml (¼ pint) full-fat milk

50 ml (2 fl oz) dry white wine (optional)

3 free-range eggs, separated

1 tablespoon French mustard

pinch of freshly grated nutmeg

pinch of cayenne pepper

fine sea salt and freshly ground black pepper

1 Place the scooped-out potato flesh in a bowl. Mix in the
spring onions, cheeses and garlic.

2 Melt the butter in a pan, quickly add the flour to make a
roux. Pour in the milk gradually to make a thick white
sauce. Add the white wine and whisk it in quickly to avoid
curdling. Bring to the boil, stirring frequently, then remove
from the heat. Whisk in the egg yolks, mustard, nutmeg and
cayenne and fold the sauce into the potato mixture.

3 Whisk the egg whites in a clean grease-free bowl until
soft peaks form. Fold carefully into the potato mixture and
season. Quickly spoon the mixture back into the potato
shells making sure they are well filled.

4 Place the potato shells on a well-oiled baking sheet and
put them quickly into a preheated oven, 160°C (325°F),
Gas Mark 6. Bake until the soufflé filling is well risen and
golden brown – about 30 minutes. Serve immediately.

Serves 4

Variations:

Insert wedges of cheese with tomatoes and fresh herbs into deep cuts made in the potatoes after cooking. Alternatively, try adding separately roasted vegetables such as aubergines, peppers, courgettes or onions.

Ring the changes by replacing ordinary baking potatoes with sweet potatoes.

Baked Potatoes

Simple yet satisfying, baked potatoes make the perfect quick family supper as a meal in themselves or as an accompaniment to another dish. The funny thing about baked potatoes is that they are so common, common knowledge about them is assumed and so certain tips as to their preparation are being forgotten.

The best potatoes for baking are all main crop, for example, Pentland Crown, Cara or King Edward.

Allow one large potato per person, about 250 g (8 oz) (young children will probably only eat a half). Wash and scrub the potato skins to remove any surface chemicals (if you can, buy organic potatoes – you'll never forget the flavour). Most importantly, once the potatoes are clean, dry them and prick with a fork. The oven should have been set to 200°C (400°F), Gas Mark 6, at which temperature a 250 g (8 oz) potato will take 50-60 minutes to cook. If you like your skins soft rub oil into them before baking. Crisp skins are achieved by adding an extra 15 minutes to the cooking time.

To serve, cut the potatoes in half, season and fork the potato flesh a little to help it absorb the topping.

Possible toppings besides butter are soured cream with chives, crème fraîche, grated vegetarian cheese, cream cheese with herbs and garlic, baked beans, barbecue beans, some of the sauces on pages 101-102 or ratatouille… in fact practically anything!

Potato Skins with Two Dips

4 large baking potatoes, scrubbed and pricked
1 tablespoon olive oil
40 g (1½ oz) butter, melted, or a little chilli oil
fine sea salt and freshly ground black pepper
TOMATO KETCHUP:
750 g (1½ lb) ripe tomatoes, roughly chopped
50 g (2 oz) demerara sugar
75 ml (3 fl oz) malt vinegar
½ teaspoon cayenne pepper
½ teaspoon paprika
1 tablespoon tomato purée
MUSTARD AND CREAM CHEESE DIP:
175 ml (6 fl oz) crème fraîche
125 g (4 oz) cream cheese
1 tablespoon snipped fresh chives
1 tablespoon wholegrain mustard, or according
  to taste

Everyone will love this as the potato skins are served with a homemade tomato ketchup and a cool creamy mustard and cheese dip.

1 To make the ketchup, place the tomatoes in a large heavy saucepan. Cover and bring gently to the boil. Remove the lid and cook quickly to allow the sauce to thicken – this will take at least 40 minutes.

2 When the sauce is thick pass it through a fine sieve and then return it to the rinsed pan. Flavour the sauce with the rest of the ingredients (the tomato purée will return the colour lost in cooking).

3 Cool, cover and refrigerate until use. (The ketchup will keep for several weeks in a clean screw-top jar or bottle in the refrigerator.)

4 To make the mustard and cream cheese dip, simply mix

all the ingredients together and chill well before serving.

5 Meanwhile, having brushed the potatoes well with olive oil, bake in a preheated oven, 190°C (375°F), Gas Mark 5, for about 1 hour or until tender. Allow to cool slightly.

6 Cut each potato into 6 wedges lengthways. Brush with melted butter or chilli oil, if using for adults. Season with salt and pepper.

7 Place under a preheated grill and grill on both sides until crisp. Serve immediately with the prepared dips.

Serves 4

Potato and Mushroom au Gratin

50 g (2 oz) butter or 3 tablespoons olive oil

250 g (8 oz) onions, finely sliced

500 g (1 lb) leeks, thinly sliced

250 g (8 oz) chestnut mushrooms, cut diagonally into
   1 cm (½ inch) slices and blanched for 30 seconds

250 g (8 oz) potatoes, peeled and thinly sliced

600 ml (1 pint) double cream

2 garlic cloves, crushed

½ teaspoon freshly grated nutmeg

50 g (2 oz) Gruyère or vegetarian Cheddar cheese,
   grated

fine sea salt and freshly ground black pepper

Sliced potatoes make an excellent topping for simple satisfying fare. The variations are endless but it's good to have at least one such dish up your sleeve that you know your children will enjoy.

This recipe uses cream but if preferred substitute with an equal quantity of white sauce – vegans can use a white sauce made with soya milk and omit the cheese.

1 Heat the butter or olive oil in a large heavy casserole dish. Add the sliced onions and cook for about 3 minutes until beginning to soften. Stir in the leeks and cook for another 5 minutes, then add the mushrooms and cook for 1 minute more.

2 Place the potatoes in a saucepan, stir in the cream, garlic, nutmeg and seasoning. Bring gently to the boil. Pour on to the onion, leek and mushroom mixture, combine well and adjust seasoning if necessary. Tip the mixture into an ovenproof gratin dish.

3 Place the dish in a large roasting tray half-filled with water and cook in a preheated oven, 180°C (350°F), Gas Mark 4, for about 1 hour, or until tender – test with a sharp knife.

4 When the potatoes are cooked, sprinkle the top with grated cheese and return to the oven until brown or gratinate under a preheated grill.

Serves 4

Pastoral Pie

BASE:

175 g (6 oz) brown lentils

3 tablespoons extra virgin olive oil

1 onion, finely sliced

2 teaspoons dried basil

1 teaspoon dried oregano

1 carrot, finely diced

1 large red pepper, cored, deseeded and finely chopped

175 g (6 oz) mushrooms, finely chopped

1 glass red wine or vegetable stock

1 tablespoon shoyu

250 ml (8 fl oz) tomato passata

3 garlic cloves, crushed

TOPPING:

500 g (1 lb) floury potatoes, peeled and quartered

500 g (1 lb) celeriac, quartered

1 egg, beaten (optional)

25 g (1 oz) butter

50 g (2 oz) vegetarian Lancashire cheese

½ teaspoon freshly grated nutmeg

fine sea salt and freshly ground black pepper

The base of this dish is something you will use time and time again. Extremely versatile, it can go under any topping or over any pasta or rice dish; it can be added to and even taken away from; best of all it is made from entirely natural and wholesome ingredients.

1 Soak the lentils overnight in cold water then cook in fresh water until almost mushy, drain and set aside.

2 Heat the oil in a deep heavy saucepan. Add the onion and herbs and cook together for 5 minutes. Add the carrot and pepper and continue to cook for a further 5 minutes.

3 Stir in the mushrooms and cook for yet another 5 minutes. Add the wine or stock and shoyu, cook gently to reduce the mixture by half before adding the passata, garlic and lentils. If the mixture is a little too thick add some more wine or water. Bring to the boil and simmer, covered, for as long as possible – at least 30 minutes. When you are happy with the flavour remove half of the mixture and roughly purée it in a liquidizer or food processor before returning it to the pan and folding it in well. Pour into a 1.8 litre (3 pint) baking dish, set aside and prepare the topping.

4 Place the potatoes and celeriac together in a large saucepan of water and cook until tender (remember that celeriac, once peeled, will oxidize unless immersed in water). Drain and mash together. Stir in the remaining topping ingredients and season well.

5 Spread the potato and celeriac mixture over the lentil base with a spatula or else pipe it on top decoratively, using a large star nozzle. Bake in a preheated oven, 200°C (400°F), Gas Mark 6, for 50-60 minutes, until the top is golden brown.

Serves 4

Variations:
There are plenty of tasty variations on the mashed potato topping. You could substitute turnips, spring greens or even apple for the celeriac. Try adding garlic and using cream or natural yogurt for a creamier topping.

French Bread and Garlic Butter Pudding

4 tablespoons extra virgin olive oil

1 large onion, finely sliced

3 tablespoons chopped fresh basil, or
  1½ tablespoons dried basil

2 tablespoons chopped fresh parsley, or
  1-2 tablespoons dried parsley

1 large aubergine cut into 2.5 cm (1 inch) cubes

6 garlic cloves, crushed

2 red peppers, cored, deseeded and cut into strips

2 courgettes, sliced

250 g (8 oz) button mushrooms, sliced

175 ml (6 fl oz) red wine

2 tablespoons tomato purée

½ tablespoon brown sugar

400 g (13 oz) can butter beans, drained

400 g (13 oz) can chopped tomatoes

50 g (2 oz) pitted black olives (optional)

1 small French stick, sliced

15 g (½ oz) Parmesan or mozzarella cheese,
  grated (optional)

fine sea salt and freshly ground black pepper

Here is a really simple dish that all the family will enjoy. It is essentially, a Mediterranean-style casserole topped with garlic bread that will tempt even the fussiest of your family. Nutritionally the dish is a perfect combination of proteins, carbohydrates, fats and vitamins.

1 Heat 2 tablespoons of the olive oil in a large casserole dish. Add the onion and sauté for 1 minute. Season with salt and pepper and add half of the herbs, if using.

2 Add the aubergine and half of the garlic and continue to cook, stirring frequently for 5 minutes. Then add the red

peppers, courgettes and mushrooms; cook for 1 further minute until the whole dish is very hot.

3 Tip in the red wine; it should immediately hiss and start to evaporate, cook gently to reduce it by half. Add the tomato purée, brown sugar, beans, tomatoes, olives and the remaining herbs, if using. Stir the mixture well and bring to a gentle simmer before covering and placing in a preheated oven, 200°C (400°F), Gas Mark 6, for 40 minutes.

4 Meanwhile, while the casserole is cooking, prepare the garlic bread. Blend the remaining olive oil with the rest of the garlic. Season with salt and pepper. Brush both sides of the sliced bread with the garlicky oil.

5 Remove the casserole from the oven. Remove the lid and inhale deeply – the smell is wonderful! Arrange the slices of garlic bread on the top of the casserole, sprinkle with Parmesan, if using, and return to the oven, uncovered, for up to 20 minutes, or until browned and slightly crisp on top.

6 Serve with a crisp salad.

Serves 4-6

Bambeano Burgers with Garlic Focaccia

BURGERS:

175 g (6 oz) black-eyed beans

125 g (4 oz) short-grain brown rice

275 ml (9 fl oz) water

1½ tablespoons extra virgin olive oil

1 large onion, finely chopped

1 green pepper, cored, deseeded and finely diced

1 teaspoon ground cumin

1 teaspoon ground coriander

¼ teaspoon chilli powder

1 tablespoon chopped fresh basil

1 tablespoon tomato purée

1 tablespoon shoyu

2 garlic cloves, crushed

a little organic wholewheat flour mixed with sesame
    seeds, for coating

fine sea salt and freshly ground black pepper

GARLIC FOCACCIA:

500 g (1 lb) unbleached strong white flour

25 g (1 oz) fresh yeast, blended with a little warm water
    and 1 teaspoon sugar

3 tablespoons olive oil, warmed, plus extra for brushing

4 garlic cloves, crushed

2 tablespoons chopped fresh oregano (optional)

coarse sea salt, for sprinkling

ITALIAN TOMATO SAUCE:

1 kg (2 lb) firm ripe tomatoes, halved

50 ml (2 fl oz) extra virgin olive oil

1 teaspoon demerara sugar or
    balsamic vinegar, to taste

This has to be the ultimate vegetarian burger recipe and will appeal to all the family, not just the children. The recipe is best made in large quantities. What is not used can be wrapped in polythene and kept frozen for up to 3 months.

I've never understood why the sesame bun is such a popular base for most burgers. At best it tastes like cotton wool, at worst it is indigestible. There are so many more exciting breads to choose from. I've chosen garlic focaccia for its flavour and soft texture. Focaccia freezes well and is best made in bulk. This recipe makes 8 good-sized buns but you may well find that half a bun is all that is really needed to go with the burgers as they are very filling.

The tomato sauce will keep refrigerated for up to a week, or can be frozen, too.

1 Cover the black-eyed beans with double their volume of cold water in a saucepan. Bring rapidly to the boil and continue to boil for 10 minutes. Remove from the heat and allow to cool before transferring to a plastic container. Let them soak for 12 hours or overnight. When ready to cook return them to the saucepan with fresh water, bring to the boil, cover and simmer for up to 1 hour or until very tender but not mushy.

2 While the beans are cooking, put the rice and water in a saucepan and bring to the boil. Simmer, covered, for up to 45 minutes, or until cooked.

3 Heat 1 tablespoon of the olive oil in a large frying pan. Add the onion, green pepper and spices and stir-fry until the onions begin to soften. Stir in the basil, tomato purée, shoyu and garlic and cook for 1 further minute.

4 Combine the cooled, cooked black-eyed beans and rice in a liquidizer or food processor. Add the vegetable mixture to this and blend it all together for a few seconds. Judge the texture according to your own preference – some may like it coarser than others. Adjust the seasoning. Divide the mixture into 8 and shape into burgers. Brush with the remaining olive oil and roll in the flour and sesame seed mixture. Chill the burgers - overnight if possible before shallow-frying for 5 minutes on each side.

5 Mix 50 g (2 oz) of the flour with the yeast liquid in a clean bowl and allow to rise for 30 minutes in a warm, draught-free place (the airing cupboard is ideal), covered with a damp tea towel.

6 Knead the remaining flour into the frothing yeast, add the warmed olive oil, the garlic and oregano, if using, as you knead the dough. Leave the dough to rise as before in a draught-free place for 1 hour, or until doubled in bulk.

7 Knock the dough back and divide into 8. Knead each piece briefly and shape into a flat bun shape. Brush with olive oil and sprinkle with coarse salt then bake in a pre-heated oven, 200°C (400°F), Gas Mark 6, for 15 minutes. Allow to cool before using.

8 To make the sauce, place the tomatoes in a saucepan with the olive oil. Cook for about 8 minutes, stirring frequently then rub the mixture through a fine sieve then adjust the flavour as you wish. If the tomatoes are very sweet add a little balsamic vinegar; if slightly bitter add demerara sugar and season with salt and pepper.

9 To serve the burgers, cut the focaccia buns in half, toast briefly, top with a freshly cooked burger, a little tomato sauce and serve with a nice, crisp salad. If liked, spread the buns with a mixture of mayonnaise and mustard and add a few slices of raw onion and may be tomato. Spread the burgers with a little French or German mustard, top with a slice of mozzarella cheese and grill until bubbling.

Makes 8

Leek and Dolcelatte Risotto

75 g (3 oz) unsalted butter

5 leeks, white parts only, cut into 5 mm (¼ inch)
   thick slices

2 teaspoons dried thyme

50 g (2 oz) ceps, sliced

6 sun-dried tomatoes, sliced

2-3 garlic cloves, crushed

175 g (6 oz) dolcelatte cheese, crumbled

2 onions, finely sliced

500 g (1 lb) arborio rice

600 ml (1 pint) dry white wine

1.2 litres (2 pints) hot vegetable stock

fine sea salt and freshly ground black pepper

TO SERVE:

4 tablespoons chopped fresh parsley or coriander

75 g (3 oz) Grana Padano or Parmesan cheese,
   grated

Arborio rice is necessary for this dish. The risotto is cooked by the absorption method and arborio grains absorb well without losing their shape or sticking together. A good risotto should always look creamy and the rice should be al dente, not overcooked.

1 Melt 40 g (1½ oz) of the butter in a large frying pan. Add the leeks and thyme and stir-fry gently for 10 minutes; the leeks should retain a lot of bite. Stir in the sliced ceps, tomatoes, garlic and dolcelatte. Allow the dolcelatte to melt over a very low heat; if it gets too hot, remove from the heat.

2 In a large saucepan heat the rest of the butter, add the onions and stir-fry for 3 minutes. Add the rice and make sure it is well coated by the butter; add a little more butter if necessary. When the rice is very hot, pour in 300 ml (½ pint) of the wine which will be absorbed very quickly, then add the rest. When this has been absorbed start adding the hot vegetable stock, a ladleful at a time.

3 When the rice is just cooked, about 15 minutes, stir in the cheese mixture and cook for a further 2 minutes before serving. Season to taste and serve, garnished with chopped parsley or coriander and grated cheese, accompanied by a fresh leafy salad.

Serves 4-6

Rigatoni with Cheesy Sun-dried Tomato Sauce

1 tablespoon extra virgin olive oil

1 large onion, finely sliced

1 small bulb of fennel, finely sliced

1 yellow pepper, cored, deseeded and finely sliced

1 fresh red chilli, deseeded and finely chopped

2 garlic cloves, crushed

1 tablespoon balsamic vinegar

1 teaspoon demerara sugar

2 tablespoons tomato purée

400 g (13 oz) can chopped tomatoes

275 ml (9 fl oz) red wine

50 g (2 oz) sun-dried tomatoes in oil, chopped

1 bunch of basil, chopped

375 g (12 oz) dried rigatoni

150 g (5 oz) mozzarella cheese, grated

25 g (1 oz) pine nuts, toasted

fine sea salt and freshly ground black pepper

To garnish:

1 sprig of mint or basil

a little grated vegetarian Pecorino cheese

This delicious sauce is definitely best made a day in advance.

1 Heat the oil in a large heavy saucepan. Add the onion, fennel, yellow pepper and chilli and stir-fry gently until the onion begins to soften. Increase the heat and add the garlic, balsamic vinegar and demerara sugar, stirring continuously. Reduce the vinegar by half then stir in the tomato purée, canned tomatoes and wine. Allow to simmer, covered, for 20 minutes.

2 Remove from the stove, cool slightly and purée in a liquidizer or food processor, or rub through a sieve. Tip into a clean container and add the sun-dried tomatoes and basil. Let their flavours infuse as the sauce cools down. At this stage it's a good idea to keep the sauce covered in a refrigerator overnight.

3 Fifteen minutes before you are ready to eat, cook the rigatoni in plenty of boiling water. Reheat the sauce and when hot stir in the mozzarella. Adjust the seasoning to taste.

4 Drain the pasta and tip into a warmed serving dish (it's a nice touch to rub the dish with a little garlic and olive oil first). Pour the sauce over the pasta, sprinkle with toasted pine nuts and garnish with sprigs of fresh mint or basil and a little grated Pecorino.

5 Serve immediately accompanied by warm Italian bread and a fresh, herby green salad.

Serves 4

Tamale Pie

lentil base (see below)

TOPPING:

125 g (4 oz) fine maize meal

1 tablespoon unbleached plain white flour

½ teaspoon salt

2 teaspoons baking powder

1 free-range egg (size 1), beaten

75 ml (3 fl oz) full-fat milk

1 tablespoon extra virgin olive oil

chopped fresh coriander, to garnish

Using the basic lentil base from the recipe for Pastoral Pie (see page 107) with the addition of 1 deseeded green chilli and a 425 g (14 oz) can red kidney beans, rinsed and drained, try this topping to make an unusual and delicious Mexican-style pie.

1 Pour the lentil base mixture into a lightly greased 18 cm (7 inch) diameter baking dish.

2 Mix all the dry topping ingredients together. Stir in the egg, milk and olive oil and mix well. Spoon the mixture over the lentil base then place in a preheated oven, 220°C (425°F), Gas Mark 7, and bake for 20-25 minutes, or until firm to the touch. Garnish with chopped coriander and serve immediately.

Serves 4

Thai Roast Tofu and Rice Noodles

250 g (8 oz) firm tofu, cubed

3 tablespoons shoyu

2 tablespoons sweet sherry, or dry sherry plus
 1 tablespoon demerara sugar

1 tablespoon mirin

1 tablespoon plus 2 teaspoons sesame oil

4 garlic cloves, crushed

1 teaspoon Szechuan chilli powder

2.5 cm (1 inch) piece of fresh root ginger, grated

250 g (8 oz) dried rice noodles

4 spring onions, cut into 2.5 cm (1 inch) lengths

250 g (8 oz) broccoli florets

250 g (8 oz) shiitake mushrooms, halved or
 left whole

250 g (8 oz) bean sprouts

3 tablespoons smooth peanut butter

50 g (2 oz) roasted peanuts, chopped

Here is a simple supper dish that uses basic ingredients to good effect. Tofu and rice noodles are both easily available from most Chinese supermarkets.

1 Place the tofu in a dish. Blend the shoyu, sherry and mirin with 2 teaspoons of the sesame oil and 2 cloves of garlic, chilli powder and the ginger. Pour this mixture over the top of the tofu and leave to marinate for 3 hours.

2 Meanwhile, cook the noodles in plenty of boiling water according to the packet instructions. Drain, cool and set aside in enough cold water to cover them (they can be kept like this for several days in the refrigerator).

3 About 30 minutes before eating remove the tofu pieces from the marinade – reserving the marinade – and place in a roasting dish. Roast in a preheated oven, 200°C (400°F), Gas Mark 6, for 25 minutes. Remove and set aside.

4 In a large heavy frying pan or wok, heat the remaining 1 tablespoon sesame oil. Stir-fry the spring onions with the broccoli florets for approximately 3 minutes. Add the mushrooms and continue to cook for a further 2 minutes. Add the remaining garlic and the bean sprouts and stir-fry for 1 minute more. Stir in the peanut butter and when it is really hot, add the reserved marinade. The sauce should instantly thicken – if it becomes too thick add a little water and adjust the seasoning accordingly.

5 Lastly, toss in the cooked noodles, roasted peanuts and the roasted tofu and heat through thoroughly before serving immediately on it's own or with a light salad or sambal.

Serves 4-6

Chestnut Mushroom and Shallot Steamed Pudding

FILLING:

50 g (2 oz) butter, or 3 tablespoons olive oil

250 g (8 oz) shallots, chopped

1 carrot, diced, or 3 baby carrots, halved

1 stick of celery, roughly chopped

1 small swede, topped, tailed, peeled and diced

2 teaspoons dried thyme

2 garlic cloves, crushed

3 tablespoons unbleached plain white flour

600 ml (1 pint) red wine or vegetable stock

2 teaspoons freshly grated horseradish (optional)

1 tablespoon wholegrain mustard

4 tablespoons chopped fresh parsley

12 chestnuts, cooked and halved

300 g (10 oz) small chestnut or button mushrooms

fine sea salt and freshly ground black pepper

PUDDING:

375 g (12 oz) unbleached plain white flour

1-2 teaspoons salt

½ teaspoon baking powder

175 g (6 oz) shredded vegetable suet

175 ml (6 fl oz) cold water

grated rind of 1 lemon

butter or vegan margarine, for greasing

1 tablespoon finely chopped fresh coriander or
   parsley, to garnish

This dish is the perfect foil for a cold winter's evening. The filling is best made 1-2 days in advance to allow the flavours to mingle.

1 To make the filling, heat the butter or oil in a large, heavy saucepan. Add the shallots and fry, covered, for 3 minutes. Add the carrots, celery, swede and thyme and continue to cook, covered, for 5 minutes.

2 Stir in the garlic, then add the flour and mix in evenly. When the whole mixture is very hot pour in the red wine or stock, gradually letting it thicken and come to the boil. When all the liquid has evaporated, reduce the heat and let the sauce simmer. Add the horseradish, mustard, parsley, salt and pepper.

3 Finally add the mushrooms and cook for 2 minutes (they must not be well cooked as they still have to survive 1-1½ hours in the steamer). Set aside to cool.

4 To make the pudding, mix the flour, salt, baking powder and vegetable suet in a bowl. Bind together with the water and knead lightly until smooth. Roll out to a round 33 cm (13 inches) in diameter. Cut a quarter out of the circle and use the larger piece to line a greased 1.8 litre (3 pint) pudding basin. Wet the overlap with water to seal the joint.

5 Pour the filling into the lined baisin.

6 Re-roll the remaining quarter of pastry into a circle to fit the top of the pudding basin. Dampen the edges with water and seal all around the edges.

7 Place a sheet of greaseproof paper and a piece of similarly sized foil over the top of the basin and secure with string as tightly as possible. Stand the basin on a heatproof saucer in the bottom of a large boiling pan. Fill the pan with enough boiling water to come about halfway up the side of the pudding basin. Cover the saucepan and boil for 1½ hours. Alternatively, place the pudding basin in an ovenproof dish or roasting tin, pour in enough water to come halfway up the side of the basin and cook in the middle of a hot oven, 200°C (400°F), Gas Mark 6, for 1½ hours.

8 To serve, carefully run a palette knife around the pudding baisin gently easing the pudding away from the sides. Place a serving dish over the top of the basin and holding firmly, invert it. The pudding should slip out easily. Garnish with chopped parsley or coriander and serve.

Serves 4-6

Dutch Pancake Stack

1 tablespoon olive oil

2 green peppers, cored, deseeded and cut into
    small strips

2 yellow peppers, cored, deseeded and cut into
    small strips

4 small courgettes, diagonally sliced

250 g (8 oz) chestnut mushrooms, sliced

2 tablespoons chopped fresh basil

250 g (8 oz) vegetarian Cheddar or mozzarella cheese,
    grated

fine sea salt and freshly ground black pepper

PANCAKES:

175 g (6 oz) organic wholewheat flour

2 teaspoons baking powder

1 teaspoon chopped fresh dill

125 ml (4 fl oz) full-fat milk

4 tablespoons cold water

50 ml (2 fl oz) soured cream

2 free-range eggs (size 4), beaten

butter, for frying

TOMATO SAUCE:

2 tablespoons olive oil

1 large red onion, finely chopped

1 teaspoon paprika

1 tablespoon red wine vinegar

1 tablespoon demerara sugar

1 tablespoon tomato purée

425 g (14 oz) can chopped tomatoes

175 ml (6 fl oz) red wine

2 garlic cloves, crushed

MUSHROOM AND TARRAGON SAUCE:

50 g (2 oz) butter

3 shallots, finely chopped

250 g (8 oz) flat mushrooms, chopped

½ teaspoon ground coriander

200 ml (7 fl oz) soured or single cream

½ tablespoon chopped fresh tarragon, or
    ¼ tablespoon dried tarragon

dash of shoyu, to taste

A stack of pancakes layered with succulent vegetables and a tasty sauce, this is a recipe guaranteed to appeal to everyone in the family, even baby. It looks and tastes great and is still unusual enough to hook the children.

The pancakes are a little more robust than normal as the recipe requires them to have some structural properties. They may be prepared up to a day in advance.

1 To make the pancakes, combine the flour, baking powder and dill in a bowl. Blend all the liquid ingredients together then add them gradually to the flour, stirring all the time. Season if you wish then set the batter aside. (Pancake batter improves with age, so if you can, make it well in advance and store in the refrigerator. When ready to use whisk the batter and add a little more water if necessary.)

2 To make the tomato sauce; heat the oil in a deep, heavy saucepan, add the onion, paprika and salt and pepper. Sauté until the onion begins to soften, add the vinegar and sugar and heat gently to reduce by half. Stir in the tomato purée, tomatoes and red wine, bring to the boil and simmer for at least 30 minutes. Add the garlic and adjust the seasoning to taste. Allow to cool and store, covered, in the refrigerator.

3 For the mushroom sauce, melt the butter in a heavy saucepan, add the shallots and sauté for about 3 minutes. Stir in the mushrooms and coriander and continue to cook for another 10 minutes over a medium heat. Pour in the cream and tarragon and gently bring back to the boil. Allow the sauce to bubble for a few minutes until the cream has reduced and thickened. Adjust the seasoning to taste and add a dash of shoyu.

4 For the vegetables, simply stir-fry them in the olive oil to the state which you like, or roast them in the oven. However you cook them, add the basil and seasoning right at the end and reserve the cheese.

5 To cook the pancakes, heat a little butter in a 23 cm (9 inch) crêpe or frying pan. Make sure that the bottom is well covered by the butter. When hot, spoon in about 3 tablespoons of the pancake batter – enough to amply cover the bottom of the pan. Reduce the heat a little and cook for 3-4 minutes until bubbles appear on the surface. Turn the pancake over and cook the other side for 1-2 minutes only.

6 Remove the pancake from the pan and place on absorbent kitchen paper. Repeat until you have 4 or 5 good pancakes. Keep any leftover batter for the next day.

7 To assemble the pancake stack, brush an ovenproof dish with melted butter. Place a pancake in the dish and cover with 1-2 tablespoons of tomato sauce. Add one-quarter of the vegetable mixture and top with the grated cheese. Make sure you spread an equal amount of vegetable mixture around the rim of the pancakes as in the middle so that the stack doesn't dip around the sides. Cover with the next pancake and repeat the process until all the pancakes, tomato sauce, vegetables and cheese are used up. You now have a very funny-looking 'cake' topped with cheese.

8 Place in a preheated oven, 200°C (400°F), Gas Mark 6, and cook for 35-40 minutes or until golden and bubbling. Meanwhile re-heat the mushroom sauce.

9 To serve, cut the pancake stack into wedges. Garnish with chopped parsley and serve with the mushroom sauce.

Serves 4

Red Pepper and Sweetcorn Fritters with Tangy Mustard Sauce

FRITTERS:

6 tablespoons extra virgin olive oil

1 onion, finely chopped

3 red peppers, cored, deseeded and finely chopped

250 g (8 oz) frozen sweetcorn, drained

250 g (8 oz) organic wholewheat flour

2 teaspoons baking powder

1 teaspoon dry mustard powder

½ teaspoon grated nutmeg

3 tablespoons finely chopped fresh parsley

2 free-range eggs, separated

300 ml (½ pint) full-fat milk

oil, for frying

SAUCE:

125 ml (4 fl oz) soured cream

2 tablespoons snipped fresh chives

½ tablespoon clear honey or mango chutney

fine sea salt and freshly ground black pepper

Anything that involves pancake batter and a frying pan is bound to be popular with the children. This is the sort of dish that comes into the category of 'special occasion or

treat'. Do not serve more than once a month although the children will want it all the time. Serve as a side dish that makes a wonderful accompaniment to grills or roasts at more adult affairs.

1 To make the fritters, heat 2 tablespoons of the olive oil in a large heavy frying pan. Sauté the onion for 3 minutes then add the red peppers and continue to sauté for 5 minutes. Stir in the sweetcorn, season and set aside to cool.

2 Sift together in a bowl the flour, the baking powder and ¼ teaspoon each of salt and pepper. Stir in the mustard powder, nutmeg and parsley and make a well in the centre.

3 Beat the egg yolks and milk together and pour this into the middle of the dry ingredients. Incorporate the liquid well to make a batter, then add the cooled vegetables.

4 Finally, beat the egg whites until stiff but not over-stiff and fold them carefully into the batter until well combined.

5 Heat a little oil in a large frying pan. Drop 1 good table-spoon of the batter into the pan and depending on the size of the pan make anything up to 6 fritters per person. Cook until golden brown – about 30 seconds each side. Keep warm in a low oven on a lightly buttered serving dish until all the fritters are cooked.

6 To make the mustard sauce combine all the ingredients together in a small bowl.

7 Serve the fritters immediately with a salad or lightly steamed vegetables and the mustard sauce. Alternatively serve with Tomato Ketchup (see page 106).

Serves 4

Lone Star Mushroom Nuggets with Campfire Sauce

SAUCE:

1 tablespoon vegetable oil

2 onions, finely chopped

½ teaspoon chilli powder

3 garlic cloves, crushed

350 ml (12 fl oz) Tomato Ketchup (see page 106)

50 ml (2 fl oz) vegetarian Worcestershire sauce

1½ tablespoons molasses

75 ml (3 fl oz) water

MUSHROOMS:

34 chestnut mushrooms, stalks carefully removed

250 g (8 oz) garlic and herb-flavoured
   cream cheese

4 tablespoons organic wholewheat flour

2 free-range eggs, beaten

50 ml (2 fl oz) full-fat milk

125 g (4 oz) organic wholewheat breadcrumbs,
   seasoned

oil, for frying

I have never been a great consumer or preparer of deep-fried foods, but if it is done conscientiously and infrequent-ly it is something for you and your family to look forward to. In this recipe stuffed mushrooms are coated in bread-crumbs, fried and served with a wonderful sauce. Mushroom nuggets freeze well and cook quite happily from frozen. Vegans can use a dairy-free pakora batter and fill their mushrooms with a mushroom duxelle.

1 Make the sauce by heating the oil in a saucepan. Add the onions, chilli powder and garlic and sauté until beginning to

soften. Add the rest of the ingredients, bring to the boil and then simmer for 5 minutes.

2 Meanwhile, fill each mushroom with cream cheese. Combine the flour, eggs and milk in a bowl to make a smooth batter. Dip the mushrooms into the batter and then quickly in the seasoned breadcrumbs. Deep-fry the mushrooms until golden brown, about 5 minutes, and serve with the sauce.

Serves 4

Calzone Carciofi

PIZZA DOUGH:

300 g (10 oz) unbleached strong white flour, plus extra
   for sprinkling
15 g (1 oz) fresh yeast
1 teaspoon demerara sugar
175 ml (6 fl oz) tepid water
1½ tablespoons extra virgin olive oil,
   plus extra for brushing

FILLING AND SAUCE:

3 tablespoons extra virgin olive oil
2 garlic cloves, crushed
425 g (14 oz) can chopped tomatoes, or
   500 g (1 lb) fresh tomatoes
10 basil leaves, torn into pieces
375 g (12 oz) mozzarella cheese, cubed
6 artichoke hearts, preserved in olive oil and
   halved horizontally
175 g (6 oz) button mushrooms, sliced
fine sea salt and freshly ground black pepper

I was amazed to discover that our children loved artichoke hearts. This discovery was made not in England but in France, at a time of year when you could stagger back from the market, your traditional carrier bag simply bursting with inexpensive globe artichokes. I thought it would be nice to include them here, although mushrooms, asparagus or indeed any favourite pizza topping can

be substituted. Calzone are excellent supper candidates because they can be totally prepared and par-cooked earlier in the day, then finished off when the hoards arrive.

1 For the pizza dough, as for making bread of any kind, try to ensure that all the equipment used is warm. Mix the flour and 1 teaspoon salt together in a large bowl. Pour some of the tepid water into a small jug. Crumble in the yeast and sugar. Cover and leave for 10 minutes in a warm place until foaming.

2 Make a well in the flour and pour in the yeast mixture and the olive oil. Mix with a fork until the water is incorporated. The dough should be smooth and pliable and readily leave the sides of the bowl. If it is too dry add more water. Knead the dough on a lightly floured surface. When soft and elastic it is ready – this will take about 10 minutes.

3 Oil a clean bowl and add the ball of dough, score its surface with a knife to help it rise and lightly sprinkle with a little flour. Cover the bowl with a damp tea towel and leave in a warm, draught-free place to double in bulk – this should take at least 1 hour.

4 Meanwhile, to make the filling and the sauce, gently heat the olive oil in a large saucepan. Add the garlic and a little seasoning and cook it without colouring. After about 1 minute add the tomatoes. Cook, taking care not to allow burning, for at least 10 minutes to reduce the canned tomato liquid slightly. Add the basil, season and set aside. (This sauce is best cooked well ahead of eating.)

5 When the dough is ready knock it back with your fist, then knead for 3 minutes before dividing into 12 equal balls. Flatten each ball with the palm of your hand then either roll or press each into a 10 cm (4 inch) round, about 2½ mm (⅛ inch) thick. Brush each circle on both sides with extra virgin olive oil.

6 Spread ½ a tablespoon of the sauce on each circle, taking care not to get it too close to the edge. Arrange half an artichoke heart and some mushrooms on the top of each, with cubes of mozzarella. Take care to arrange the vegetables and cheese on one half of each circle only.

7 Fold over the other half of the circle and pinch the edges together to form a half moon shape. Sprinkle the calzone with flour (or cornmeal, if preferred) and place on a floured baking sheet. Bake in a preheated oven, 220°C (425°F), Gas Mark 7, for 20 minutes, or until golden brown.

8 Serve with the remaining sauce and a nice crisp salad.

Makes 12 x 10 cm (4 inch), or 2 x 28 cm (11 inch) calzone

Hot Lentil and Cheshire Cheese Salad

250 g (8 oz) Puy lentils, washed

1.8 litres (3 pints) water

3 garlic cloves, crushed

1 bouquet garni

1 carrot, peeled and diced

3 shallots, finely chopped

fine sea salt and freshly ground black pepper

DRESSING:

6 tablespoons extra virgin olive oil

2 tablespoons balsamic vinegar

1 tablespoon Dijon mustard

3 garlic cloves, crushed

1 tablespoon snipped fresh chives

2 teaspoons chopped fresh chervil

SALAD BASE:

250 g (8 oz) fresh ripe tomatoes, skinned, deseeded and chopped

1 bunch of spring onions, chopped

2 gem lettuces, pulled apart

2 red peppers, cored, deseeded, roasted and torn into strips

½ curly endive, roasted and torn into strips

½ oakleaf lettuce, roasted and torn into strips

250 g (8 oz) Cheshire cheese, cut into 1 cm (½ inch) cubes

1 tablespoon chopped fresh parsley

12 ripe black olives, to garnish (optional)

This salad is a wholesome meal in itself and a swift but unusual answer to a family's needs at the end of the day. Puy lentils are truly king amongst lentils but they do require careful washing. This salad contains everything a growing family could want and vegans can substitute cubes of pan-fried tofu for the cheese.

1 There is no need to soak the lentils overnight but do rinse and drain them. Place in a saucepan with the water, garlic, bouquet garni, carrot, shallots and seasoning. Bring to the boil then simmer until tender, about 40 minutes.

2 While the lentils are cooking, combine all the dressing ingredients thoroughly and assemble the salad base without the cheese or tofu, if using, and parsley in a salad bowl.

3 When the lentils are cooked add three-quarters of the dressing, the cheese and the parsley to them. Pour the rest of the dressing over the salad in the bowl then top this with the lentils. Garnish with black olives and serve.

Serves 4

Family Stew and Dumplings

250 g (8 oz) dried mixed beans (butter beans,
   kidney beans, flageolets or borlotti beans)

1 tablespoon extra virgin olive oil

1 large onion, finely sliced

1 large leek, finely sliced

125g (4 oz) carrots, chopped

125 g (4 oz) celeriac, chopped

125 g (4 oz) parsnip, chopped

1 red pepper, cored, deseeded and cut into strips

125 g (4 oz) mushrooms, sliced

1 dessertspoon demerara sugar

1 dessertspoon red wine vinegar

425 g (14 oz) can chopped tomatoes

1 tablespoon tomato purée

1 teaspoon yeast extract, dissolved in
   300 ml (½ pint) boiling water

2 tablespoons torn basil leaves

1 bay leaf

DUMPLINGS:

75 g (3 oz) self-raising flour

½ teaspoon salt

25 g (1 oz) vegetarian suet

15 g (½ oz) vegetarian Cheddar cheese, grated

1 tablespoon chopped fresh parsley

1 tablespoon chopped fresh thyme

fine sea salt and freshly ground black pepper

Family stews tend to evolve, look at this as a starter recipe and see how yours develops over the years. Family stews can be topped with a wide range of toppings – here I've chosen dumplings.

1 Soak the mixed beans overnight. Boil them rapidly in fresh water for about 10 minutes then simmer until tender, about 50-60 minutes. Drain the beans well.

2 Heat the oil in a large casserole dish. Add the onion and leek and cook for 3 minutes. Add the rest of the vegetables except the mushrooms and cook for a further 5 minutes. Add the mushrooms, sugar and wine vinegar, simmer gently and reduce the liquid by half.

3 Stir in the tomatoes and tomato purée and bring to the boil. Add the beans and the water and bring the casserole to a gentle simmer before stirring in the basil, bay leaf and season to taste.

4 Cover the casserole, transfer to a preheated oven, 180°C (350°F), Gas Mark 4, for at least 1 hour.

5 Meanwhile, make the dumplings. Combine the flour and salt together in a bowl, rub in the suet until the mixture resembles breadcrumbs. Add enough cold water to form a firm dough.

6 Knead the grated cheese, fresh herbs and seasoning into the dough then break into pieces and form into walnut-sized dumplings.

7 When the stew has been in the oven for 40 minutes remove it and dot the surface with the dumplings. Replace the lid and allow the stew to cook for at least a further 20 minutes. Serve hot.

Serves 4

FUNDAMENTAL SWEETS

On good days fundamental desserts follow fundamental suppers. Here are several simple desserts that you can make very quickly. My wife, Kate, has a very sweet tooth and for her no meal is complete without something sweet to round it off – even savoury toast has to be followed by a ripe peach or apricot!

Cold Chocolate Fondue

CHOCOLATE SAUCE:

125 g (4 oz) good-quality dark or white chocolate, broken into pieces

175 ml (6 fl oz) single cream, or water if vegan

1½ tablespoons demerara sugar

FRUIT:

125 g (4 oz) fresh strawberries, hulled

125 g (4 oz) fresh pineapple, cubed

125 g (4 oz) ripe nectarine, cut into wedges

125 g (4 oz) fresh cherries, pitted

125 g (4 oz) Ogen melon, cubed

125 g (4 oz) seedless grapes

2 tablespoons lemon juice

Sounds exotic but this is a simple and popular way of serving a fruit salad. Once again, only use chocolate containing more than 35% cocoa solids. For a dinner party add a little kirsch or schnapps to the chocolate sauce, if liked.

1 To make the chocolate sauce, melt the chocolate in a bowl set over a saucepan of boiling water. Add the sugar to the melted chocolate. Allow to cool for 5 minutes, then stir in the cream or water.

2 To serve, equip the family with cocktail sticks, a bowl of sauce and the freshly prepared fruit and watch it disappear! Small chewy meringues are excellent accompaniments.

Serves 4

Strawberry Ice Cream

250 g (8 oz) rhubarb, trimmed and chopped

250 g (8 oz) fresh strawberries, hulled and chopped

50 g (2 oz) demerara sugar

juice of 2 oranges, at least 125 ml (4 fl oz)

1 teaspoon ground ginger

425 g (14 oz) can condensed milk

750 ml (1¼ pints) Greek yogurt

As a popular dessert nothing is quicker than ice cream so why not have a go at making your own? Allow 20 minutes for defrosting once it is out of the freezer.

1 Place the chopped fruit, sugar, orange juice and ground ginger in a large heavy saucepan, bring to the boil and then simmer until very tender, stirring occasionally, 10 minutes. Remove the pan from the heat and allow to cool then blend in a liquidizer or food processor until really smooth. Alternatively, rub through a sieve.

2 Stir in the condensed milk and yogurt, mixing well to form a good smooth texture. Pour the mixture into a shallow plastic freezer container and place in the freezer. Stir vigorously every 30 minutes while it is freezing.

3 When totally frozen wrap in cling film and keep frozen until needed.

Serves 4

Quick Raspberry and Ginger Cheesecake

BASE:

250 g (8 oz) ginger biscuits, crushed

125 g (4 oz) unsalted butter, melted then cooled

FILLING:

150 ml (¼ pint) double cream

250 g mascarpone cheese

2 tablespoons clear honey

juice of 1 lime

375 g (12 oz) raspberries or strawberries

One thing that really annoys me is cheesecakes set with gelatine or agar agar. What a ghastly substance to combine with succulent fruit and fresh dairy produce! Baked cheesecakes, I find a bit on the dry side – I like cheesecake to be firm but moist and to taste all the way through like this one.

1 Make the base by combining the melted butter and the crushed biscuits and pressing them into a greased 20 cm (8 inch) flan tin with a removable bottom. Chill for at least 30 minutes.

2 For the filling, whip the cream in a bowl until firm but not stiff, then add the mascarpone, beating it into the cream to a smooth texture. Fold in the honey and lime juice and most of the raspberries or strawberries, reserving a few for decoration.

3 Spoon the cheese mixture on to the chilled biscuit base and smooth the surface over with a spatula. Chill for at least 3 hours and just before serving decorate with the reserved raspberries.

Serves 4

Pear and Banana Scotch Pancakes

8 Scotch pancakes or drop scones

25 g (1 oz) unsalted butter

2 pears, peeled, cored and quartered

2 teaspoons ground cinnamon

2 tablespoons clear honey

juice of ½ orange

2 tablespoons lemon juice

2 bananas, halved lengthways then halved across widthways

4 tablespoons crème fraîche, cream or soured cream

Good-quality Scotch pancakes are easily available for a quick dessert – you probably would not have time to make them yourself – and go well with quickly cooked fruits.

1 Melt the butter in a large frying pan. Add the pears and cinnamon and cook gently for 4 minutes. Stir in the honey, orange and lemon juice and bananas and cook for a further 5 minutes.

2 Meanwhile, toast the Scotch pancakes under a preheated grill, allowing 2 per person. When ready, place on warmed plates topped with the fruit and a spoonful of crème fraîche or cream.

Serves 4

Banoffee Crumble Cake

BASE:

425 g (14 oz) can condensed milk, unopened

250 g (8 oz) sweet shortcrust pastry, chilled (see page 130)

3 large bananas, sliced and dipped in lemon juice and water

TOPPING:

125 g (4 oz) unsalted butter

125 g (4 oz) organic wholewheat flour

125 g (4 oz) demerara sugar

50 g (2 oz) regular oats

50 g (2 oz) mixed chopped nuts

1 teaspoon ground mixed spice

Here's a variation on Banoffee Pie which is good hot or cold and excellent served with fresh custard or cream.

1 Make the toffee well in advance by boiling the unopened can of condensed milk in a saucepan of water for 3 hours, remembering to keep the water topped up. Remove the can from the water and allow to cool slightly before opening carefully. The evaporated milk will have become a thick caramel-coloured toffee.

2 Roll out the chilled pastry using very little excess flour. Try to only roll in one direction, until it is about 2.5 mm (⅛ inch) thick.

3 Lightly brush a 23 cm (9 inch) flan dish with oil and line it with the pastry, trimming off any excess. Prick the bottom with a fork. Line the pastry case with greaseproof paper and fill with baking beans – ceramic ones if possible. Place in a preheated oven, 190°C (375°F), Gas Mark 5, for about 10 minutes or until the pastry is just beginning to colour. Remove the baking beans and allow the flan case to cool.

4 Meanwhile, to make the topping, rub the butter into the flour in a bowl until it resembles fine breadcrumbs, stir in the rest of the ingredients.

5 Line the par-cooked flan case with the sliced bananas, top with the toffee. Sprinkle the crumb topping over this and lightly smoothing all over. Return the flan to the oven and bake for 20-25 minutes until golden brown.

6 Serve with crème fraîche or cream.

Serves 4

Sweet Shortcrust Pastry

125 g (4 oz) organic wholewheat pastry flour, sift but retain bran

pinch of salt

50 g (2 oz) golden caster sugar

50 g (2 oz) unsalted butter or vegan margarine at room temperature

2 free range egg yolks - vegans can use 2 tablespoons soya flour, plus more water

There are many variations of this recipe - but few use organic wholewheat flour. The technique of sifting out the bran and adding it back later on is one which will hold good for almost all forms of pastry, bread and cake making.

1 Sift the flour and salt on to a clean and cold surface (marble is best). Make a well in the centre. Add the sugar, butter, egg yolks and bran, if using. Using your fingertips work the ingredients together until they are well mixed to form a soft but not sticky dough. It may be necessary to add a little water - definitely, if making the bran version.

Makes enough for a 9 inch flan dish

Tofu and Blueberry Brûlée

1 tablespoon kirsch (optional)

250 g (8 oz) fresh, thawed frozen or drained, canned blueberries

250 g (8 oz) silken tofu

1 tablespoon maple syrup

½ teaspoon vanilla extract

50 g (2 oz) mixed nuts, lightly toasted

125 g (4 oz) demerara sugar

This dish is equally good for vegans and will cook well using any soft fruit or even poached hard fruit.

If using the kirsch, which adults particularly will enjoy, marinate half of the blueberries in the kirsch.

1 Blend the tofu, the maple syrup, vanilla extract and 125 g (4 oz) of the plain blueberries in a bowl until smooth.

2 Reserve 8 of the remaining blueberries, whether marinated or not, and divide the rest among 4 ramekins. Top with the smooth tofu mixture. Sprinkle with the toasted mixed nuts and chill well for about 1 hour.

3 Meanwhile, melt the sugar in a small heavy saucepan. When dissolved and a caramel colour, pour a thin layer on to the top of each ramekin. Chill again for 1 hour.

4 Serve, decorated with the reserved blueberries.

Serves 4

Rhubarb, Gooseberry and Lemon Steamed Pudding

FILLING:

250 g (8 oz) demerara sugar, according to taste

300 ml (½ pint) water

750 g (1½ lb) fresh gooseberries, topped and tailed

grated rind and juice of 1 lemon

SPONGE:

125 g (4 oz) unsalted butter

125 g (4 oz) golden caster sugar

½ teaspoon vanilla extract

2 free-range eggs, beaten

1 free-range egg yolk

175 g (6 oz) self-raising flour

juice and finely grated rind of ½ lemon

After a very simple main course it's always nice to stun the family by magically producing a steamed pudding. Steamed puddings are generally made during winter months with winter fruit such as apples and pears but I've never known anyone turn one down even in midsummer! Frozen gooseberries and almost any other fruit can be substituted for the fresh gooseberries.

If you have a microwave this is a truly instant dessert. Use 2 pudding basins or halve the ingredients. They will only take 5-8 minutes to cook on a high setting, depending on the power of your machine.

1 Boil the sugar and water together in a heavy saucepan to make a syrup. Add the gooseberries and poach them gently until tender but not mushy. Set aside.

2 Half-fill a large saucepan with water and bring to the boil. Grease a 900 ml (1½ pint) pudding basin with butter.

3 Cream the butter and sugar together in a bowl until light and fluffy in texture. Add the vanilla extract, then gradually beat in the eggs and egg yolk.

4 Using a metal spoon, carefully fold in the flour, the lemon juice and rind.

5 Spoon most of the gooseberries into the prepared pudding basin then cover with the sponge mixture – there should be enough to come three-quarters of the way up the sides of the basin.

6 Cover the baisin with buttered foil and secure with string. Place in the pan of boiling water. Reduce the heat to a simmer. Cover and cook for 1½ hours.

7 When cooked invert the pudding on to a plate and spoon any excess gooseberry 'syrup' over it. Serve with cream, crème fraîche or real custard.

Serves 4

FAMILY FEASTS

Traditional family feasts tend to centre on a prized 'lump' of meat. How many times do you hear people boasting about their Sunday joint: 'it was huge, you should have seen it!' – almost as if they had reared the animal themselves. Not wanting to feel left out, vegetarians have devised similar 'lumps' for themselves like nut roast, with which you can have all the trimmings.

In this chapter we have 'feasts' in the true spirit of the family, feasts which the family share, both physically and socially. These feasts are for conversing and for enjoying each other's company. By necessity they are flexible feasts, easily expanded upon, and some can expand outdoors into the garden.

Of all the countries in the world England seems to be forgetting its family feasts. Only 20 miles across the English Channel family eating is still the very cornerstone of society. In France the family includes not only Mum, Dad and 2.4 children but also grandparents, aunties, uncles, cousins, good friends and sometimes people just passing by. Most families get together if not daily then certainly weekly; food is shared and problems discussed. Where have we gone wrong? Throughout the world families are eating together - one can instantly name Italians, Indians, Chinese, Spanish and Liverpudlians, so what's happened to us? At the end of the day we are too busy. Even if it's only once a week get your family together - if you haven't got family get friends - communication is vital for our society.

FEAST ONE

The riot of colour, texture and taste of Mexican food occurred when the Spanish cookery culture imposed itself on the tranquil but refined tastes of a highly developed Indian culture in South America.

Today Mexican food is becoming more and more popular especially as a family food. Avoid using hot chillies there are plenty of cool ones to choose from!

Serves 4

Mexican Fajitas and Frijoles
Tomato and Coriander Salsa

Tijuana Fruit Salsa

Mexican Fajitas and Frijoles

FLOUR TORTILLAS:

300 g (10 oz) unbleached plain white flour

1 teaspoon fine sea salt

50 g (2 oz) white vegetable fat

150-175 ml (5-6 fl oz) warm water

FRIJOLES:

175 g (6 oz) dried black kidney beans, or
   650 g (1 lb 5 oz) can pinto or red kidney beans

1 bay leaf

1 tablespoon virgin olive oil

1 red onion, chopped

3 garlic cloves, crushed

1 red chilli, finely chopped (deseeded for
   a milder dish)

fine sea salt and freshly ground black pepper

sprigs of basil, to garnish

VEGETABLE FILLING:

2 large onions, sliced

1-2 red chillies, finely chopped

3 garlic cloves, crushed

juice of 2 limes

2 tablespoons chopped fresh coriander

4 large red peppers, cored, deseeded and cut
   into strips

4 large yellow peppers, cored, deseeded and cut
   into strips

4 large courgettes cut into thin strips

2 tablespoons extra virgin olive oil

fine sea salt and freshly ground black pepper

2 tablespoons chopped fresh coriander or
   basil, to garnish

DIPS:

2 ripe avocados

juice of 1 lime

300 ml (½ pint) soured cream

1 bunch of chives, finely snipped

This translates as 'Little packages and refried beans' accompanied by avocado and lime dip, soured cream and chives and salsa.

It is a wonderful family dish so long as you don't go too mad on the chillies. Any food that involves participation at the meal table apart from normal eating with a knife and fork always seems to be automatically successful. Children and parents alike will enjoy assembling their own food in this vegetarian version of a Mexican favourite.

Ensure that everyone is seated, relaxed and ready for the dish to arrive, while you cook the vegetables, as they are best eaten hot and tend to cool quite quickly. If possible, keep them warm in a dish over a candle or a spirit burner.

Frijoles is a traditional Mexican dish sometimes called Refritos (Refried Beans). It is actually best made in advance and re-heated, giving the flavours a chance to develop. It will keep well for up to 4 days, covered, in a refrigerator. Frijoles are commonly made with black kidney beans but red kidney beans and pinto beans are equally tasty although not quite so eye-catching.

1 To make the tortillas, put flour and salt in a bowl, rub in the fat to form a crumb-textured mixture. Slowly add the warm water, mixing in to form a soft dough.

2 Place the dough on a lightly floured surface and knead for 1 minute. Divide into 12 pieces and cover with a damp cloth to prevent it from drying out. Roll out each piece into a 15 cm (6 inch) diameter circle. Dust off any excess flour and stack on a plate placing a piece of kitchen paper between each tortilla.

3 Heat a heavy frying pan until very hot – cure it with salt if necessary to prevent sticking. (See note below.) Cook the tortillas for 1 minute on each side or until patchy-brown. It may be necessary to wipe the pan between tortillas to avoid any excess flour burning. Once cooked place them in an ovenproof dish covered with a damp cloth to keep them moist.

4 If using dried beans for the frijoles, put them in a deep saucepan and cover with double their volume of water, bring to the boil quickly then boil rapidly for 10 minutes. Set the beans aside and allow to soak overnight or for at least 12 hours.

5 Put the beans into fresh water with the bay leaf, bring to the boil, cover and simmer for 1-1½ hours, or until very tender but not mushy. While they are cooking, heat the oil

in a pan. Add the onion, garlic and chilli and fry until the onion has softened – be careful not to burn them.

6 Drain the cooked beans, reserving the cooking liquid, and add to the onion mixture, or add the canned beans, if using, instead. Mash with a potato masher adding a little of the bean cooking liquid to make a moist consistency (don't use a food processor here as the resulting purée would be disappointing). Season and set aside to cool.

7 For the vegetable filling, combine all the ingredients in a bowl, cover and allow to marinate in the refrigerator overnight. Ten minutes before serving, remove the vegetables from the marinade and place in a hot frying pan and stir-fry for 5-6 minutes, or until the onions are starting to soften – if it's a bit dry add a little of the marinade.

8 For the two dips, simply scoop out the flesh of the avocados, add the lime juice, season and place in a serving dish. Combine the soured cream and chives and serve in another dish.

9 To serve the meal, re-heat the beans in a low oven, a microwave or, even better, refry them and serve in a dish garnished with basil sprigs. The tortillas may be re-heated in a hot oven or in a steaming basket. Place the dips, beans and tortillas on the table and serve the vegetables.

10 To assemble, place a hot tortilla on your plate, add some vegetables, a good dollop of frijoles and top with any combination of the accompaniments. Simply roll it up and enjoy it! The meal could be stretched with the addition of salads, nachos, cheese or even a rice dish, all washed down with Mexican beer for the adults and perhaps fresh lime and lemonade for the children.)

Note:

To cure a frying pan with salt, heat the pan until hot. Add salt to cover the bottom of the pan and using kitchen paper, rub into the pan until clean. Wipe the pan and use.

Overleaf Left- MEXICAN FAJITAS AND FRIJOLES Right- TIJUANA FRUIT SALSA

Tomato and Coriander Salsa

1 small red onion, finely chopped
2 tablespoons chopped fresh coriander
2 garlic cloves, crushed
250 g (8 oz) fresh, ripe tomatoes, skinned,
    deseeded and chopped
a dash of white wine vinegar and/or brown sugar,
    to taste
fine sea salt and freshly ground black pepper
coriander leaves, to garnish

1 Combine the onion, coriander, garlic and a small amount of the tomatoes in a liquidizer or food processor and blend for about 10 seconds. Then fold the mixture into the rest of the tomatoes, season and adjust the acidity. If it is too sweet, add a little white wine vinegar; if too sharp, add a little brown sugar.
2 Pour the salsa into a serving dish, season and garnish with coriander leaves. Serve as an accompaniment to Fajitas and Frijoles (see page 134).

Tijuana Fruit Salsa

1 small ripe pineapple, cut into 1 cm (½ inch) cubes
1 ripe mango, skinned, stoned and cubed
1 ripe banana, sliced
4 passion fruits, pulp of
1 small ripe Galia melon, cut into chunks
2 tablespoons fresh lime juice
4 tablespoons fresh orange juice
4 mint leaves

After a filling and spicy main course tastebuds cry out to be cleansed and cooled. This dessert has a truly tropical feel and is excellent served with vanilla ice cream or smooth and creamy Greek yogurt.
1 Combine the fruit and fruit juices in a glass serving bowl well in advance to allow the flavours to mingle. Serve well chilled and garnish with fresh mint.

FEAST TWO

Latkes are the most simple of all pancakes made most commonly from mashed potato. They are generally accredited to northern Europe, Poland, Germany and Russia in particular but are made in one form or another throughout the world. (There are wonderful street vendors in Morocco that sell tiny potato pancakes flavoured with garlic, fried in olive oil and served with a searing hot chilli sauce.) Like all good food forms they will adjust to seasons, climates and may be added to and accompanied by a myriad of different things and what is most important, is the context of this book, in that the children will love them!

These spinach latkes, accompanied by a delicious wild mushroom and cheese sauce and followed by a sumptuous dessert is the perfect meal for any type of gathering; be it family or friends.

Serves 4

Spinach Latkes with Wild Mushroom and Three-Cheese Sauce

Sticky Apple and Lemon Pudding

Spinach Latkes with Wild Mushroom and Three-Cheese Sauce

LATKES:

3 tablespoons extra virgin olive oil

4 shallots, finely sliced

2 teaspoons mustard seeds

2 carrots, grated

250 g (8 oz) fresh spinach, stalks removed and chopped

500 g (1 lb) mashed potato

1 teaspoon lemon juice

fine sea salt and freshly ground black pepper

SAUCE:

25 g (1 oz) butter

375 g (12 oz) mushrooms (such as oyster mushrooms, chanterelle or plain flat mushrooms)

600 ml (1 pint) double cream

175 g (6 oz) Fontina cheese, cut into small pieces

75 g (3 oz) Gorgonzola cheese, cut into small pieces

2 garlic cloves, finely chopped

1 tablespoon chopped fresh basil

50 g (2 oz) Parmesan cheese, grated

Latkes can be made a day in advance and stored uncooked in the refrigerator separated by small squares of greaseproof paper.

1 To make the latkes, heat 2 tablespoons of the olive oil in a large saucepan. Cook the shallots until beginning to soften. Add the mustard seeds and allow to pop; stir in the carrots and spinach and cook until soft. If you can, try to evaporate as much of the water from the spinach as possible, stir continuously to avoid burning.

2 When the carrots are cooked but still have some 'bite' remove from the heat and fold in the mashed potato, lemon juice and seasoning to form an even consistency. Let the mixture cool.

3 Using floured hands shape the mixture into 8 round patties.

4 Heat enough of the remaining oil in a saucepan and fry the latkes for 5 minutes on each side until golden brown.

5 For the sauce, heat the butter in a heavy frying pan, add the mushrooms, season with salt and pepper and cook for about

5 minutes. Remove the mushrooms from the pan with a slotted spoon and set aside. Over a high heat reduce the liquid left in the pan to a spoonful.

6 In a separate saucepan bring the cream to a gentle boil and let it reduce by half. Reduce the heat to very low and add the Fontina, Gorgonzola, garlic and basil. Finally, stir in the mushrooms, reduce the liquid a little more. Adjust the seasoning and just before serving add the Parmesan.

7 Serve the latkes with a wedge of lemon and a nice crisp salad and/or some plainly cooked vegetables and, of course, the sauce.

Sticky Apple and Lemon Pudding

125 g (4 oz) unsalted butter

1 kg (2 lb) cooking apples, peeled, cored
    and chopped

50 g (2 oz) raisins

2 heaped tablespoons light muscovado sugar

dash of rum (optional)

125 g (4 oz) demerara sugar

3 free-range eggs (size 1), separated,
    the yolks beaten

1 teaspoon ground cinnamon

grated rind and juice of 2 lemons

2 tablespoons unbleached self-raising white flour

pinch of salt

½ teaspoon cream of tartar

150 ml (¼ pint) milk

whipped cream, to serve

This is a moisturising pudding, although the addition of fresh whipped cream or crème fraîche will make it a feast.

1 Melt 50 g (2 oz) of the butter in a heavy saucepan, add the apples, raisins, muscovado sugar and a dash of rum, if using. Stir-fry for 2 minutes then transfer the mixture to a 20 cm (8 inch) soufflé dish. Allow to cool.

2 Beat the remaining butter and demarara sugar together in a bowl until light and fluffy. Gradually add the egg yolks. When the mixture is well combined stir in the ground cinnamon, lemon juice and rind. Sift in the flour with the salt, cream of tartar and then slowly add the milk. Mix until the mixture is smooth.

3 Whisk the egg whites in a clean, grease-free bowl until soft peaks form then fold into the rest of the mixture. Pour over the apples and place straight into a preheated oven, 180°C (350°F), Gas Mark 4. Cook until well risen and firm to the touch, about 40-50 minutes. Serve with whipped cream.

FEAST THREE

Cooking with the season is no longer the prerequisite it was, even 50 years ago. But when cooking this meal do try to use fruit and vegetables that are in season. August/September would be ideal in England when peppers are plump and sweet, and peaches (almost) ripe and juicy and still warm from their trees in Southern Europe. It is a perfect meal after a long hot summer day. What ever you do don't tell the children it is goat's cheese until they have finished eating it!

Serves 4

Warm Italian Roast Salad with Goats' Cheese and Croûtons

Italian Peach Tart

Muscat Zabaglioni

Warm Italian Roast Salad with Goats' Cheese and Croûtons

1 large yellow pepper, cored, deseeded and cut into
   thick strips

1 large green pepper, cored, deseeded and cut into
   thick strips

6 shallots, peeled and trimmed

a little dried thyme or oregano, for sprinkling

3 garlic cloves, crushed

6 tablespoons extra virgin olive oil, plus extra
   for brushing

2 tablespoons white wine vinegar

1 dessertspoon demerara sugar

6 tomatoes, skinned, deseeded and cut into strips

3 tablespoons chopped fresh basil

250 g (8 oz) organic white spirelli pasta

175 g (6 oz) goats' cheese, crumbled

175 g (6 oz) garlic croûtons

12 olives, halved and pitted

fine sea salt and freshly ground black pepper

Here's a salad that's a meal in itself. 'Roast salad', I hear you say – sounds a bit improbable. Read on and all will be revealed.

1 Brush the peppers and shallots with a little olive oil. Season with salt and pepper and some thyme or oregano, if liked. Place in a roasting dish in a preheated oven, 220°C (425°F), Gas Mark 7, for 30-40 minutes or until tender.

2 Meanwhile, mix together the garlic, the 6 tablespoons of oil, the vinegar, sugar and seasoning in a bowl. Stir in the tomatoes then gently stir in the basil.

3 Cook the spirelli in a large saucepan of boiling water until *al dente*. Drain and combine immediately with the tomato and basil dressing. Add the warm peppers and shallots, then top with the goats' cheese, warm garlic croûtons and the olives.

4 Serve with chunks of fresh Italian bread or grilled polenta.

Overleaf Left- WARM ITALIAN ROAST SALAD WITH GOATS CHEESE AND CROÛTONS *Right-* ITALIAN PEACH TART

Italian Peach Tart

150 g (5 oz) unsalted butter

125 g (4 oz) filo pastry

200 g (7 oz) mascarpone cheese

125 g (4 oz) cream cheese

½ teaspoon vanilla extract

2 tablespoons clear honey

rind and juice of 1 small lime

1 kg (2 lb) peaches, skinned if like, stoned and
   thickly sliced

2 tablespoons Moscato white wine

50 g (2 oz) chocolate shavings, to decorate

*A light main dish demands a substantial dessert like this
one. Try this tart using any orchard fruit. Choose peaches
that are firm, yielding very slightly, unblemished and not
over-ripe.*

1 Gently melt 50 g (2 oz) of the butter and brush some on
to the bottom of a 23 cm (9 inch) loose-based fluted flan
tin; lay a sheet of filo pastry over it. Brush the pastry sheet
with more melted butter and then lay another sheet of
pastry on top. Repeat this process until all the filo has
been used.

2 Line the pastry case with greaseproof paper and fill with
ceramic baking beans. Bake blind in a preheated oven,
200°C (400°F), Gas Mark 6, for 10 minutes before
removing the beans and greaseproof paper. Brush the pastry case with more butter and finish cooking, about another 5-6 minutes. Set aside to cool.

3 Meanwhile, mix together the mascarpone, cream
cheese, vanilla extract, honey, lime juice and rind in a
small bowl.

4 Melt the remaining butter in a large frying pan. Sauté
the peaches for about 3 minutes then add the wine and
reduce it to a thick syrup. Cook the peaches over a high
heat until caramelized and almost dry.

5 Spread the cream cheese mixture over the filo pastry
base and top with the peaches. Decorate with chocolate
shavings and serve warm or chilled with whipped cream or
crème fraîche.

Muscat Zabaglioni

3 free range egg yolks

45 g (1½ oz) golden caster sugar

60 ml (2 fl oz) Muscat wine

150 ml (¼ pint) double cream

*The perfumed sweetness of Muscat is the perfect accom-
paniment to peaches or other fruity desserts. Muscat
Zabaglioni can be also be served as a dessert in its own
right. It is no more difficult to make than custard.*

1 In a heatproof bowl beat the egg yolks with the sugar
until pale and fluffy.

2 Put the bowl above a saucepan of boiling water and
gradually add the wine whisking frequently. When the
sauce has thickened without curdling set it aside to cool.

3 Whisk the cream until it forms soft peaks then beat in
the Muscat sauce. Chill well before serving.

FEAST FOUR

This recipe is guaranteed to capture your children's attention. Your main problem will be getting them to slow down and eat at a pace which allows the rest of the family to have some. There should be penalties for dropping bits of bread or vegetables in the fondue (especially washing up or stacking the dishwasher) - like wise for dripping fondue on to the tablecloth.

Serves 4

Herby Fondue
Celeriac and Carrot Salad

Chocolate Coffee Cake

Herby Fondue

25 g (1 oz) butter

1 small onion, chopped

25 g (1 oz) unbleached plain white flour

250 ml (8 fl oz) full-fat milk

1 tablespoon chopped fresh basil

1 tablespoon chopped fresh parsley

1 tablespoon chopped fresh chervil

1 tablespoon snipped fresh chives

125 ml (4 fl oz) dry white wine

250 g (8 oz) Gruyère cheese, grated

250 g (8 oz) Emmental or Edam cheese, grated

1 tablespoon brandy or kirsch

finely grated nutmeg

pinch of cayenne pepper

1 garlic clove, peeled and halved

fine sea salt and freshly ground black pepper

TO SERVE:

750 g (1½ lb) crusty bread, cut into 2.5 cm (1 inch) cubes

300 g (10 oz) cooked vegetables (such as cauliflower or
  broccoli florets, carrot sticks, celery, peppers or
  new potatoes)

Another 'doing dinner' – this is probably really only suitable for children over 8 although of course you can set aside little bits of cool fondue for your younger ones. It will help to have fondue equipment for this dish – earthenware sets are best.

1 Melt the butter in a deep heavy saucepan. Add the chopped onion and cook until beginning to soften. Stir in the flour and cook for about 1 minute. Gradually stir in the milk to make a white sauce. Season to taste.

2 Stir the herbs into the sauce then gradually add the white wine, being careful not to curdle the sauce. Add the remaining ingredients except the garlic. Rub the inside of your fondue dish with the cut garlic and pour in the fondue. Keep warm over a spirit burner.

3 Serve, using fondue forks to dip the bread and vegetables into the fondue.

Celeriac and Carrot Salad

250 g (8 oz) carrot, coarsely grated

I small celeriac, peeled and cut into julienne strips

75 g (3 oz) lexia raisins (large and sweet)

50 g (2 oz) toasted pumpkin seeds

DRESSING:

3 tablespoons freshly squeezed lemon juice

75 ml (3 fl oz) sunflower oil

3 teaspoons clear honey

I tablespoon Dijon mustard

75 ml (3 fl oz) mayonnaise

fine sea salt and freshly ground black pepper

Celeriac is a lovely vegetable it just looks ugly, best raw and young it still tastes good old and cooked. Apart from salads, soups and stews it is great as a side dish in its own right.

1 Make the dressing, combine the lemon juice, oil, honey and seasoning in a screw top jar.

2 Fold the Dijon mustard into the mayonnaise.

3 Quickly toss the grated carrot and celeriac strips in the lemon and honey dressing. It should be moist and not wet.

4 Fold in the raisins and toasted pumpkin seeds into the mixture and finally add the mustard mayonnaise.
Refrigerate the salad at least 30 minutes before serving.

Chocolate Coffee Cake

250 g (8 oz) plain chocolate, broken into pieces

I tablespoon instant coffee granules

250 g (8 oz) golden caster sugar

5 eggs, separated

250 g (8 oz) ground almonds

TOPPING:

300 ml (½ pint) whipping cream, whipped

I tablespoon dark rum

sifted cocoa powder, for sprinkling

After a rich main course sometimes the only flavour that can fight back is chocolate. Chocolate and coffee make an excellent partnership.

1 Melt the chocolate in a heatproof bowl over a large heavy saucepan of gently boiling water, whisk in the instant coffee granules and remove from the heat.

2 Cream the sugar and egg yolks together in a bowl until light and fluffy. Stir in the almonds, melted chocolate and coffee. Beat well together.

3 Whisk the egg whites in a clean grease-free bowl until stiff then fold into the chocolate and coffee mixture. Pour into a greased 23 cm (9 inch) cake tin and bake in a pre-heated oven, 170°C (350°F), Gas Mark 4 for 55 minutes until firm to the touch. Leave for a few minutes before turning out on to a wire rack.

4 When cool top with the whipped cream into which a little rum has been beaten and sprinkle the cake with the sifted cocoa powder.

Makes a 23 cm (9 inch) cake

FEAST FIVE

This feast would make a lovely Sunday lunch or brunch as it is healthy and the children will love it. Grilled asparagus might be a new experience for British children but it's an old art form in the USA. Boston Beans are my favourite way of cooking beans and probably were the first vegetarian dish I ever cooked.

Serves 4

Ranch-Style Rösti
Boston Baked Beans
Grilled Asparagus

Muffled Plums
Treacle Sauce

Ranch-Style Rösti

500 g (1 lb) Maris Piper potatoes
250 g (8 oz) celeriac
125 g (4 oz) vegetarian Cheddar cheese, grated
2 tablespoons extra virgin olive oil
2 teaspoons chopped fresh thyme
2 tablespoons chopped fresh parsley
½ teaspoon cayenne pepper
4 free-range eggs (size 1)
fine sea salt and freshly ground black pepper

1 Par-cook the potatoes and celeriac in a large pan of salted boiling water for 10 minutes. Drain, cool and peel, then grate into a bowl. Stir the cheese into the potatoes, then add the oil, herbs and seasoning.
2 Spoon the mixture into a lightly oiled baking dish or 4 individual ovenproof dishes – do not compress the mixture. Make 4 slight hollows in the potato, if using one large dish. Bake in a preheated oven, 200°C (400°F), Gas Mark 6, for 20 minutes then remove and break an egg into each dish or the hollows in the one dish. Return to the oven for a further 10 minutes or until the eggs have just set. Serve immediately.

Boston Baked Beans

500 g (1 lb) dried borlotti beans
1 large onion, chopped
2 sticks of celery, chopped
4 garlic cloves, crushed
1 green chilli, chopped
1 bay leaf
2 cinnamon sticks
2 tablespoons molasses
1 tablespoon demerara sugar
3 tablespoons tomato purée
3 tablespoons wholegrain mustard
3 tablespoons malt vinegar
fine sea salt and freshly ground black pepper
2 tablespoons chopped fresh parsley, to garnish

Best cooked and prepared a day ahead, these make excellent accompaniments to all manner of main dishes and are good on their own, with bread and salsa. They take quite a lot of cooking

Overleaf Left- GRILLED ASPARAGUS, BOSTON BAKED BEANS *Right-* RANCH-STYLE RÖSTI

so make plenty and freeze what you don't use. If borlotti beans are unavailable, haricot and kidney beans are good substitutes.

1 Bring the beans to the boil in a large saucepan of water. Cook rapidly for 10 minutes, skim them if necessary then simmer for 45 minutes or until tender.

2 Drain the beans and place in a casserole dish. Add the rest of the ingredients to the beans, cover and bake in a preheated oven, 150°C (300°F), Gas Mark 2, for about 4 hours or until soft, thick and saucy. Serve the beans hot or cold.

Grilled Asparagus

20 asparagus stalks (grade 1)

3 tablespoons extra virgin olive oil

2 tablespoons lemon juice

fine sea salt and freshly ground black pepper

Once again the children surprisingly love asparagus and tuck into it with gusto when offered. If preferred, steam the asparagus and serve with a simple lemon butter sauce.

1 Brush the asparagus with some of the olive oil, making sure that each stalk is well coated and season to taste. Grill slowly under a low heat for about 5 minutes or until the tip of a knife inserted tells you they are done.

2 Serve the asparagus with more fruity olive oil and a splash of lemon juice.

Muffled Plums

175 g (6 oz) butter, softened

175 g (6 oz) golden caster sugar

1 teaspoon ground ginger

500 g (1 lb) cooking plums or greengages, halved and pitted

2 free-range eggs (size 1), beaten

125 g (4 oz) unbleached white self-raising flour

1 teaspoon baking powder

50 g (2 oz) regular oats

1 teaspoon ground cinnamon

3 tablespoons milk

In this case 'muffle' has many applications but most of all it's the noise you make when you're eating them! Any fruit or combination of fruit, especially orchard fruit, could be used in place of the plums.

1 Melt 50 g (2 oz) of the butter with 50 g (2 oz) of the sugar and the ginger together in a small saucepan.

2 Place the plums in a 1.2 litre (2 pint) shallow ovenproof dish and pour the melted butter, sugar and ground ginger over them.

3 Beat the remaining butter and sugar together in a bowl until light and fluffy, gradually add the eggs then fold in the flour, baking powder, oats and cinnamon. Finally beat in the milk. Spread the mixture over the plums. Bake for about 30 minutes in a preheated oven, 190°C (375°F), Gas Mark 5, until firm to the touch.

4 Serve hot with fresh vanilla custard, cream, ice cream or Treacle Sauce (see below).

Treacle Sauce

40 g (1½ oz) butter

125 g (4 oz) light muscovado sugar

1 tablespoon molasses

75 ml (3 fl oz) double cream

1 Heat the butter, sugar and molasses together in a small saucepan until melted, then stir in the cream. Bring the mixture to the boil gently and allow to reduce to a thick creamy consistency.

FEAST SIX

Have your very own vegetarian Balti supper or lunch at home. The essence of a 'Balti' meal is two contrasting curries served not with rice but with naan bread to scoop up mouthfuls of the delicious curry. Once again this will be a guaranteed success with the whole family and if the older members prefer a bit more spice than the younger ones then it's easy just to make another more spicy dish specifically for them.

Traditionally Balti food comes from Baltistan, a remote part of Pakistan. The food was cooked in woks, which it is believed were inherited into the culture of the wandering Baltis from the Chinese. It's nice to use the traditional individual iron Balti dishes for your meal but they will act more as serving receptacles than as a means of cooking.

Serves 4

Red Onion and Mint Raita
Naan Bread
Balti Sauce
Medium Aubergine and Potato Balti
Mushroom and Courgette Korma

Mango Kulfi

Red Onion and Mint Raita

2 red onions, finely chopped

pinch of chilli powder

squeeze of lemon juice

4 tablespoons chopped fresh mint

1 tablespoon chopped fresh coriander

1 teaspoon mustard powder

1 teaspoon ground cumin

½ teaspoon finely grated fresh root ginger

250 ml (8 fl oz) Greek yogurt, stirred

50 ml (2 fl oz) soured cream

fine sea salt and finely ground black pepper

8 poppadums, to serve

Just something for dipping poppadums into, to nibble on while waiting for the main dish to arrive.

1 Mix all the ingredients together well and chill before serving, accompanied by the poppadums for dipping into the raita.

Naan Bread

15 g (½ oz) demerara sugar

20 g (¾ oz) fresh yeast

300 ml (½ pint) tepid milk

65 g (2½ oz) butter

500 g (1 lb) unbleached strong white flour

1 teaspoon sea salt

1 tablespoon chopped fresh coriander

Overleaf Left- RED ONION AND MINT RAITA, NAAN BREAD *Right-* MANGO KULFI, MEDIUM AUBERGINE AND POTATO BALTI, MUSHROOM AND COURGETTE KORMA.

Normally cooked in a tandoori oven, a similar result can be achieved at home with a hot grill.

1 Mix the sugar and yeast in a small jug with 100 ml (3½ fl oz) of the warm milk. Cover and set aside in a warm place for 10 minutes until frothing.

2 Meanwhile, rub 50 g (2 oz) of the butter into the flour and salt in a bowl and melt the remaining butter, setting it aside. When the yeast is frothy add it to the flour mixture and gradually add the rest of the milk. Mix well to form a dough. Put it on to a lightly floured work surface and knead for 10 minutes. Place in an oiled bowl, cover the bowl with clingfilm and place in a warm, dry, draught-free place for 1 hour or until doubled in bulk.

3 Knock back the dough and divide into 4. Roll each piece out into a large rough thin circle. Prick all over with a fork and press the coriander into the surface.

4 Heat a baking sheet under a hot grill. When hot place a naan on it and grill for a few minutes each side until just started to brown. Brush with the melted butter, wrap in foil and keep warm in a low oven while cooking the rest. Naan bread are best served warm.

Balti Sauce

3 red onions, finely chopped

3 garlic cloves, crushed

2 green chillies, deseeded and chopped

2.5 cm (1 inch) piece of fresh root ginger, grated

4 tablespoons ghee, or melted skimmed butter

1 teaspoon mustard powder

1 teaspoon ground fenugreek

½ teaspoon ground cumin

1 tablespoon ground turmeric

½ tablespoon paprika

1 tablespoon ground coriander

1 teaspoon ground cinnamon

5 whole cardamoms, crushed

5 whole cloves

grated rind and juice of 1 lemon

3 tablespoons tomato purée

600 ml (1 pint) water or vegetable stock

fine sea salt and freshly ground black pepper

This is the key to Balti entertaining – a sauce which can be added to almost anything.

1 In a large heavy saucepan fry the onions, garlic, chillies and ginger in the ghee or butter for 8 minutes. Add the spices and stir-fry for 1 minute. Add the remaining ingredients, bring to the boil and simmer for 45 minutes.

2 Pass the sauce through a fine strainer and adjust the seasoning to taste. Allow to cool then store in the refrigerator until ready to use. It will keep for several days.

Makes 600 ml (1 pint)

Medium Aubergine and Potato Balti

1 onion, sliced

1 tablespoon fennel seeds

1 tablespoon black mustard seeds

3 tablespoons ghee or vegetable oil

500 g (1 lb) aubergines, cut into chunks

2 red peppers, cored, deseeded and cut into
   2.5 cm (1 inch) squares

250 g (8 oz) green beans, topped, tailed, halved
   and blanched

375 g (12 oz) new potatoes, cooked and halved

175 g (6 oz) okra, blanched

1 quantity Balti Sauce (see opposite)

375 g (12 oz) tomatoes, skinned, deseeded
   and chopped

25 g (1 oz) fresh sweet basil, chopped

fine sea salt and freshly ground black pepper

1 In a large saucepan, fry the onion and seeds together in the ghee or oil until the seeds pop. Add the aubergine and cook for 5 minutes. Add the peppers, beans, potatoes and okra and cook for a further 10 minutes.

2 Stir in the Balti sauce and bring to the boil. Fold in the chopped tomatoes and basil, adjust the seasoning to taste and cook for a further 4 minutes, before ready to serve.

Mushroom and Courgette Korma

1 onion, chopped

2 tablespoons ghee, or melted skimmed butter

750 g (1½ lb) button mushrooms

¾ quantity Balti Sauce (see page 154)

75 g (3 oz) creamed coconut

50 g (2 oz) ground almonds

425 g (14 oz) courgettes, topped, tailed and sliced

150 ml (¼ pint) double cream

4 tablespoons chopped fresh coriander

fine sea salt and freshly ground black pepper

50 g (2 oz) flaked almonds, toasted, to garnish

This is a startling contrast to the previous dish! Use the tiniest mushrooms you can find.

1 In a saucepan fry the chopped onion in the ghee over a high heat for 1-2 minutes, add the mushrooms and cook for a further 3 minutes.

2 Stir in the Balti sauce, creamed coconut and ground almonds and bring to the boil. Add the sliced courgettes and cook gently for a further 8 minutes. Stir in the cream and cook for a further 2 minutes. Add the coriander and seasoning and serve garnished with the flaked almonds.

Mango Kulfi

300 g (10 fl oz) single cream

50 g (2 oz) golden caster sugar

5 green cardamoms, crushed

grated rind of 1 lemon

1 large ripe mango, about 425 g (14 oz), peeled and stoned

50 g (2 oz) pistachio nuts, chopped, to garnish

I think that this is one of the nicest ice creams in the world! Vegans could use soya milk and extra sweetener in place of the single cream.

1 Warm the cream in a small saucepan together with the sugar, cardamoms and lemon rind. As soon as the sugar dissolves, remove the pan from the heat. Allow the mixture to cool and infuse, then strain.

2 In a liquidizer or food processor blend the mango and cream together to a smooth texture. Pour into a shallow freezerproof plastic container and freeze for about 1½ hours. Stir the mixture after this time – it should be beginning to freeze. If desired, pour the kulfi into cleaned yogurt pots. Return to the freezer until frozen solid.

3 Serve the kulfi garnished with the chopped pistachios.